Pan Study Aids

GW00502874

Maths

F. G. J. Norton

Pan Books London and Sydney
in association with **Heinemann Educational Books**

First published 1980 by Pan Books Ltd,
Cavaye Place, London SW10 9PG
in association with Heinemann Educational Books Ltd
   6 7 8 9
ISBN 0 330 26079 0
© F. G. J. Norton 1980
Printed and bound in Great Britain by
Richard Clay (The Chaucer Press) Ltd, Bungay, Suffolk

PAN STUDY AIDS

Titles published in this series

Accounts and Book-keeping
Advanced Biology
Advanced Chemistry
Advanced Mathematics
Advanced Physics
Biology
British Government and Politics
Chemistry
Commerce
Economics
Effective Study Skills
English Language
French
Geography 1   *Physical and Human*
Geography 2   *British Isles, Western Europe, North America*
German
History 1   *British*
History 2   *European*
Human Biology
Maths
Physics
Sociology
Spanish

Brodies Notes on English Literature

This long established series published in Pan Study Aids now
contains more than 150 titles. Each volume covers one of the
major works of English literature regularly set for examinations.

Contents

Preface

This book is designed to give the student a sound guide for revision before the G.C.E. Ordinary Level examinations. It emphasizes the most important points, which are those frequently tested in the examination, and gives general advice how a candidate can use his knowledge efficiently to do himself justice. Each section begins by clarifying the topic, then has some worked G.C.E.-type examples, and finally some questions of examination standard for the student to do himself. The answers to these are given at the back of the book.

There is still some variation between G.C.E. syllabuses, although many Boards now have a 'common core' syllabus and have reduced the width of the syllabuses they offered in the early 1970s. Students should consult up-to-date syllabuses at school, college, or in the local Public Library, and are advised to cross out topics in this book that are not in the syllabus they are offering. Booklets of past G.C.E. papers set by the Board can be obtained from each Board, and should be studied with the exercises in this book. Students preparing for an examination with multiple-choice questions should obtain practice in answering these, and may find 'Objective tests in Ordinary Level Mathematics' by F. G. J. Norton and L. Harwood Clarke (London: Heinemann, 1969) helpful.

I should like to thank Hamish MacGibbon, Graham Taylor, and all at Heinemann Educational Books for their help in seeing to the production of the book; my pupils, for their enthusiastic advice and comments; and my family for their constant readiness to discuss ideas with me, and especially Eleanor Norton, for reading the manuscript and commenting on it.

Rugby, 1980   F. G. J. Norton

General examination hints

1 **Read the questions carefully**, especially all the *numbers* given. What is the scale given for the graph questions?

2 Try to **choose your questions carefully**; in particular, start with a question you can do. It is most unlikely that you *must* start with question 1.

3 Always **make a rough estimate of any calculation**. If you are using a calculator, set out each calculation clearly so that you (and the examiner) can see what you are trying to do.

4 **Draw a diagram** if the question is at all complicated. 'One picture is worth a thousand words'.

5 Always **try to keep solutions as simple as possible** – if you find a difficult method, you may make a mistake in following it! For example, when solving isosceles triangles, draw the perpendicular bisector of the 'base'; do not use the sine or cosine formula.

6 **Do not cross out an answer** because you think that it is wrong. Part of your solution may well be right, and you will lose the marks for this if you cross out the attempt.

7 If you have finished before the end of the examination, **check your work carefully**.

8 If you are 'stuck' in one question, **check that you have used all the information given**, and see whether you can get any ideas from any earlier part of the question that you have already answered.

1 Arithmetic

Summary of arithmetical terms

The **natural numbers** 1, 2, 3, 4, . . . are those used for counting; they are also sometimes called **whole numbers** or the **cardinal numbers**.

The **positive integers** are natural numbers greater than 0, i.e. 1, 2, 3, 4, . . . The set of all positive integers is sometimes denoted by Z_+, i.e. $Z_+ = \{1, 2, 3, 4, \ldots\}$.
The set of **all integers** is denoted by Z, i.e. $Z = \{\ldots, -4, -3, -2, -1, 0, 1, 2, 3, 4, \ldots\}$.
N.B. 0 is an integer but not a positive integer.

Rational numbers are those obtained by dividing an integer by another integer, e.g. $\frac{3}{4}$. The set of all rational numbers is denoted by Q, i.e. $Q = \{\ldots, -\frac{3}{4}, \ldots, -\frac{1}{8}, \ldots, \frac{1}{4}, \ldots\}$.
All the numbers that we come across at this stage are *real* numbers, denoted by **R**. Numbers such as $\sqrt{-1}$ are not real numbers.

Numbers that are not rational, but can be the roots of algebraic equations, e.g. $\sqrt{2}$, are called **irrational**. Those numbers, e.g. $\pi, \pi + 1$, π^2, that cannot be the roots of such equations are called **transcendental** numbers.

The numbers are represented by numerals (usually in **base** ten); the numerals may contain several digits, e.g. 345 has three digits. In base ten, 345 represents the number $3 \times 100 + 4 \times 10 + 5$.

In a fraction, e.g. $\frac{3}{4}$, the number on the top line is called the **numerator**, here 3; and the number on the bottom, here 4, the **denominator**. If the numerator and the denominator have a common factor we can divide by that factor, e.g. $\frac{6}{8} = \frac{3}{4}$.

In a **proper** fraction the numerator is less than the denominator, e.g. $\frac{3}{4}$ is a proper fraction but $\frac{5}{4}$ is an **improper** fraction.   A decimal is a fraction whose denominator is a power of ten, e.g. $0.7 = \frac{7}{10}$.

A number is **prime** if the number has no factors other than 1 and the number itself. It follows from this definition that 1 is **NOT** prime.

The **highest common factor** (h.c.f.) of two numbers is the largest number that is a factor of each, e.g. the h.c.f. of 75 and 120 is 15. The **lowest common multiple** (l.c.m.) of two numbers is the smallest number of which both numbers are factors, e.g. the l.c.m. of 75 and 120 is 600.

Counting numbers

As we count sheep, we use a different number, one, two, three, four, at each stage to record how many sheep have passed, and if we write

Fig. 1.1

down these numbers we use *numerals* to denote them. We shall probably use the Arabic numerals 1, 2, 3, 4, ... and, if we use a

Babylonian

| Y | YY | YYY | YYY Y | YYY YY | YYY YYY | YYYY YYY | YYYY YYY YY | YYYY YYYY | ◄ | ◄◄ | ◄◄◄ | ◄◄◄◄ | ◄◄◄◄◄ | 7 |

Roman

| I | II | III | IV | V | VI | VII | VIII | IX | X | XX | XXX | XL | L | LX |

Arabic

| 1 | 2 | 3 | 4 | 5 | 6 | 7 | 8 | 9 | 10 | 20 | 30 | 40 | 50 | 60 |

different numeral for each number, we shall have to devise a system to prevent ourselves running out of numerals.

We can group the sheep into fives (as we do with tally-marks), and record how many fives we have . . .

Fig. 1.2

We can group in dozens (12) and gross (144) using base twelve, or scores (20), but, as we probably intend to use numerals in base ten, it will be simplest if we group the sheep in tens. We have one group of ten and three left over. The number 'thirteen' is represented by

Fig. 1.3

the numeral 13, which signifies one group of ten, and three extra. Use is made of the position of each digit, its 'place value', so that 123 signifies one group of 'ten tens', two groups of 'ten', and three extra; similarly for all other numerals in base ten.

Fig. 1.4

We do not of course need to draw all one hundred and twenty three sheep before we can divide them into groups of specific sizes.

Successive division by 5 gives

$$
\begin{array}{r}
5)123 \\
24 \quad \text{remainder 3} \\
5)\,24 \\
4 \quad \text{remainder 4}
\end{array}
$$

so that we have four groups of 'five-fives', four groups of 'five', and three extra, that is

$$123 = 4 \times (5 \times 5) + 4 \times 5 + 3,$$

i.e. $123_{ten} = 443_{five}$

Example 1.1 *Express* 88_{ten} *in base three.*

$$
\begin{array}{ll}
3)88 & \\
3)29 & \text{remainder 1} \\
3)\ 9 & \text{remainder 2} \\
3)\ 3 & \text{remainder 0} \\
1 & \text{remainder 0}
\end{array}
$$

We have found that

$$88 = 1 \times (3)^4 + 0 \times (3)^3 + 0 \times (3)^2 + 2 \times 3 + 1,$$

so $88_{ten} = 10\ 021_{three}$

Example 1.2 *Express* 419_{ten} *in base twelve, using the symbols t for ten and e for eleven.*

Dividing as before,

$$
\begin{array}{l}
12)419 \\
12)\ 34 \text{ remainder 11, written } e \text{ base twelve} \\
2 \text{ remainder 10, written } t \text{ base twelve}
\end{array}
$$

So $419 = 2 \times (12)^2 + 10 \times 12 + 11,$

i.e. $419_{ten} = 2te_{twelve}$

Addition and subtraction in bases other than ten

The arithmetic operations of addition and subtraction are carried out in exactly the same manner as in base ten, but we have to take extra care when 'carrying' or 'borrowing', since this requires using the number base.

Example 1.3 *The numbers being in base eight, subtract 54 from 73.*

$$
\begin{array}{r}
73 \\
54- \\
\hline
\end{array}
$$

As we begin the subtraction, we notice that 4 is greater than 3, so that we also have to use one of the groups of eight to subtract 4 from 13_{eight}, that is, 4 from eleven, so

$$73$$
$$54-$$
$$\overline{1\not9}$$

Multiplication and division

The method for multiplication and division is again the same as for base ten, but care must be taken to recall and apply correctly the new tables.

Example 1.4 *Both numbers being in base eight, multiply* 413 *by* 5.

Notice that when multiplying by 5, $5 \times 3 = 17_{\text{eight}}$, $5 \times 4 = 24_{\text{eight}}$ so that we have 1 or 2 to carry, thus $413 \times 5 = 2467$.
Similarly, to multiply 413 by 55 if all numbers are in base eight

$$
\begin{array}{r}
413 \\
55 \times \\
\hline
24670 \\
2467 \\
\hline
27357
\end{array}
$$

So $\qquad 413 \times 55 = 27\,357$

Binary numbers

The commonest base other than ten is two, and numbers written in this base are called *binary* numbers. Multiplication and division are particularly easy in base two, as we can only multiply by 1 or 0.

Example 1.5 *Find the product of the binary numbers* 101 *and* 11 011.

$$
\begin{array}{r}
11011 \\
101 \\
\hline
1101100 \\
11011 \\
\hline
10000111
\end{array}
$$

Example 1.6 *Divide* 10 000 110 *by* 111.

$$\begin{array}{r} 10011 \\ 111\overline{)10000110} \\ 111 \\ \hline 1011 \\ 111 \\ \hline 1000 \\ 111 \\ \hline 1 \end{array}$$

So the quotient is 10 011 and the remainder is 1.

Octal numbers

Binary numbers do become very long; octal numbers, which are about one-third of the length of binary numbers and easily converted into binary numbers, can often be used instead. Each digit in an octal number converts into a trio of binary digits (including zeros), and vice-versa.

Example 1.7 *Express the binary number* 1 101 111 100 *as an octal number, and the octal* 73 *in binary.*

Since
$$101 = 5, \; 111 = 7, \text{ and } 100 = 4$$
$$1 \; 101 \; 111 \; 100_{two} = 1574_{eight}$$
and
$$73_{eight} = 111 \; 011_{two}$$

Properties of numbers

One advantage of studying numbers written in bases other than ten is that we realize the reason for some of the simple properties of numbers. For example, to test whether a number written base ten is divisible by 9, we find whether the sum of the digits is divisible by 9. Suppose the number is written $abcd$, then

$$\begin{aligned} abcd_{ten} &= a \times 10^3 + b \times 10^2 + c \times 10 + d, \\ &= a \times (999 + 1) + b \times (99 + 1) + c \times (9 + 1) + d, \\ &= 999a + 99b + 9c + (a + b + c + d), \\ &= 9(111a + 11b + c) + (a + b + c + d), \end{aligned}$$

so that, if 9 is a factor of $(a + b + c + d)$, then it is a factor of *abcd*. We can easily devise similar tests for divisibility in other bases (*see* Exercise 1a, questions **7, 8, 9**).

Example 1.8 *What number base is being used, if* $432 + 654 = 1306$?

Since the sum of 2 and 4 in this number base is 6, and the digit 6 anyway occurs in one of the given numbers, we know that the base must be greater than 6. But $3 + 5$ can only equal 10 if the base is eight, and checking, $4 + 6 + 1 = 13$ only in base eight. The base used therefore is eight.

Exercise 1a

1 Express the following base ten (denary) numbers in (a) base two, (b) base three, (c) base eight, (d) base twelve, using t for ten and e for eleven:

$$5, 7, 9, 13, 23, 24, 48, 64, 96$$

2 Express the following binary numbers in base ten:

$$11, 101, 1010, 1100, 11\,000, 111\,000$$

3 Express the following numbers base three in base ten:

$$21, 221, 2021, 1000, 2000$$

4 Express the following binary numbers as octals:

$$11, \ 111, \ 1000, \ 11\,000, \ 1\,000\,000$$

5 Express the following octal numbers as binary:

$$11, \ 111, \ 13, \ 100, \ 137$$

6 In each of the following, what number base has been used?

(a) $214 + 562 = 1106$, (b) $357 - 161 = 176$, (c) $132 \times 2 = 304$.

7 How can you tell at a glance that a binary number is divisible by four?

8 How can you tell at a glance that an octal number is divisible by four?

9 How can you tell that an octal number is divisible by 7?

10 (a) List the seven positive binary whole numbers which have not more than three digits.

    (b) How many positive whole numbers in base three have not more than three digits?

    (c) Answer the same question for numbers base (i) four, (ii) ten.

    (d) Deduce from your answers above how many positive whole numbers in base n have not more than three digits.

Decimals

In the same way that we use the place of a digit to indicate the power of ten by which it is multiplied, we can, having introduced a decimal marker (usually a point . though a comma , is used in some countries) place the digits to the right of that marker to indicate the power of ten by which the number is divided. Thus

$$0.2 = \frac{2}{10}, \ 0.13 = \frac{13}{10^2} = \frac{13}{100} \text{ and } 0.004 = \frac{4}{10^3} = \frac{4}{1000}$$

These decimals are manipulated in the same way as numbers without a decimal marker, though care must be taken to see that the decimal marker is positioned correctly.

Example 1.9 *Find the value of* (a) $(0.2)^2$, (b) $(0.4)^2$, (c) $(0.2)^3$, (d) $\frac{0.6}{0.2}$, (e) $\frac{0.04}{0.2}$.

(a) $(0.2)^2 = 0.2 \times 0.2 = \frac{2}{10} \times \frac{2}{10} = \frac{4}{100} = 0.04$
(b) $(0.4)^2 = 0.4 \times 0.4 = \frac{4}{10} \times \frac{4}{10} = \frac{16}{100} = 0.16$
(c) $(0.2)^3 = 0.2 \times 0.2 \times 0.2 = \frac{2}{10} \times \frac{2}{10} \times \frac{2}{10} = \frac{8}{1000} = 0.008$
(d) Since a fraction is unaltered if the numerator and denominator are multiplied by the same number,

$$\frac{0.6}{0.2} = \frac{6}{2} = 3$$

(e) $\frac{0.04}{0.2} = \frac{4}{20} = \frac{2}{10} = 0.2$

When decimals are multiplied together, the number of digits to the right of the decimal marker in the product is equal to the sum of the number of digits to the right of the marker in the numbers being multiplied together. Care should be taken of any final zeros in the product,

e.g. $0.2 \ \times 0.03 \ = 0.006 \quad (1 + 2 = 3)$
            $0.02 \times 0.004 = 0.000 \ 08 \ (2 + 3 = 5)$
but $0.02 \times 0.005 = 0.000 \ 10 \ (2 + 3 = 5,$ though a fifth digit only occurs in the product if we retain the zero on the far right, obtained from $2 \times 5 = 10$.)

A similar rule can be devised for division, though it is almost invariably easier to avoid division by a decimal by multiplying numerator and denominator by a suitably large power of ten, e.g.

$$\frac{0.005}{0.02} = \frac{0.5}{2} = 0.25$$

and

$$\frac{0.108}{0.0004} = \frac{1080}{4} = 270$$

Example 1.10 *Simplify* $\dfrac{(0.5)^2 + 2}{0.09}$

Work out the bracket first: $(0.5)^2 = 0.25$

So

$$\frac{(0.5)^2 + 2}{0.09} = \frac{2.25}{0.09}$$

Multiply numerator and denominator of the fraction by 100:

$$\frac{(0.5)^2 + 2}{0.09} = \frac{2.25}{0.09} = \frac{225}{9} = 25$$

Fractions

To share a bar of chocolate fairly with a friend, we divide it into two halves. To share with two friends we divide it into thirds: to share with three friends, into quarters. The idea of these easy fractions is familiar to us all. To manipulate them, though, we need a few simple rules.

Addition and subtraction of fractions

In a fraction, say $\frac{3}{4}$, we call the term on the top line, here 3, the **numerator**, and the term on the bottom line, here 4, the **denominator**. The denominator tells us into how many parts the whole has been divided; the numerator tells us how many of those parts we are now considering.

To add $\frac{1}{5}$ to $\frac{2}{5}$, we notice that the denominators are the same, so that both fractions refer to the same sized parts of a whole, here, fifths. We can therefore add the parts, $\frac{1}{5} + \frac{2}{5} = \frac{3}{5}$.

If the denominators are not the same, then we must express each fraction in a form with equal denominators, which will be the l.c.m.† of the denominators. Thus $\frac{1}{5} + \frac{7}{10} = \frac{2}{10} + \frac{7}{10} = \frac{9}{10}$, and $\frac{2}{3} - \frac{1}{2} = \frac{4}{6} - \frac{3}{6} = \frac{1}{6}$.

† Lowest common multiple, the smallest number into which every denominator divides. (*See also* p. 10.)

Example 1.11 *Find the value of (a)* $\frac{1}{3} + \frac{1}{4} + \frac{1}{6}$, *(b)* $2\frac{2}{3} - 1\frac{5}{6}$.

(a) The l.c.m. of 3, 4, and 6 is 12, so we write each fraction with a denominator 12. Thus

$$\tfrac{1}{3} + \tfrac{1}{4} + \tfrac{1}{6} = \tfrac{4}{12} + \tfrac{3}{12} + \tfrac{2}{12} = \tfrac{9}{12} = \tfrac{3}{4}$$

(b) We can consider the whole numbers separately, and subtract 1 from 2 to give 1. When we come to the fractions, though, we see that $\frac{2}{3} - \frac{5}{6} = \frac{4}{6} - \frac{5}{6} = -\frac{1}{6}$

Thus we have $2\frac{2}{3} - 1\frac{5}{6} = 1 + (\frac{2}{3} - \frac{5}{6}) = 1 - \frac{1}{6} = \frac{5}{6}$, (using $1 = \frac{6}{6}$).

Multiplication of fractions

If a bar of chocolate has been divided into thirds, and each piece is then halved, we have six equal pieces, each one-sixth of the whole. Thus $\frac{1}{2}$ of $\frac{1}{3}$ is $\frac{1}{6}$. More generally, we have

$$\frac{a}{b} \times \frac{c}{d} = \frac{ac}{bd}$$

This result only applies to fractions, not to mixed numbers like $3\frac{1}{2}$.

Thus $\qquad \frac{2}{5} \times \frac{3}{4} = \frac{6}{20} = \frac{3}{10}$ and $\frac{5}{6} \times \frac{2}{5} = \frac{10}{30} = \frac{1}{3}$

Division of fractions

The value of a fraction is unaltered if the numerator and denominator are multiplied by the same number, so that

$$\frac{\frac{2}{3}}{\frac{3}{4}} = \frac{\frac{2}{3} \times 4}{3} = \frac{\frac{8}{3}}{3} = \frac{8}{9}$$

This can be summarized by saying that the fraction which is the divisor should be inverted, and then multiplication carried out. But it is much clearer if we ignore that rule, and think merely of multiplying numerator and denominator at each stage, as above, instead of

$$\frac{\frac{2}{3}}{\frac{3}{4}} = \frac{2}{3} \times \frac{4}{3} = \frac{8}{9}$$

Example 1.12 *Simplify* $\dfrac{\frac{2}{5}}{\frac{3}{8}}$—

$$\frac{\frac{2}{5}}{\frac{3}{8}} = \frac{\frac{2}{5} \times 8}{3} = \frac{16}{3 \times 5} = \frac{16}{15}$$

Binary fractions, bicimals

If we are using numbers base ten, then the places after the marker denote the powers of ten by which the numerator is divided. This idea can be extended to the binary and other scales, so that in binary

$$0.1 = \frac{1}{2}, 0.01 = \frac{1}{2^2} = \frac{1}{4}, 0.001 = \frac{1}{2^3} = \frac{1}{8}, \text{ etc.}$$

To write a (denary) fraction as a bicimal, if the denominator is a power of two we have only to express both numerator and denominator as binary numbers, then division is easy, thus

$$(\tfrac{7}{8})_{ten} = (\tfrac{111}{1000}) = 0.111_{two}$$

Fractions with other denominators require repeated division in binary, the same method that is used when expressing denary fractions as decimals. These bicimals only terminate if the denominator is a power of 2.

Example 1.13 *Express $\frac{2}{5}$ as a binary fraction.*

$$(\tfrac{2}{5})_{ten} = (\tfrac{10}{101})_{two}$$

Divide
$$
\begin{array}{r}
0.01100110 \\
101)\overline{10.000000} \\
1.01 \\
\hline
110 \\
101 \\
\hline
1000 \\
101 \\
\hline
110 \\
101 \\
\hline
10
\end{array}
$$

The sequence recurs, so that $(\tfrac{2}{5})_{two}$ as a bicimal is $0.011\ 001\ 100\ 11\ldots$, i.e. $0.0\dot{1}10\dot{1}$

Example 1.14 *Express the bicimal 0.1101 as a fraction base ten.*

Since $0.1 = \frac{1}{2}, 0.01 = \frac{1}{4}, 0.001 = \frac{1}{8}$, and $0.0001 = \frac{1}{16}$
$$0.1101 = \tfrac{1}{2} + \tfrac{1}{4} + \tfrac{1}{16}$$
$$= \tfrac{8}{16} + \tfrac{4}{16} + \tfrac{1}{16} = \tfrac{13}{16}$$

Exercise 1b

1 Find the value of (a) $(0.3)^2$, (b) $(0.7)^2$, (c) $\dfrac{0.7}{0.2}$, (d) $\dfrac{0.7}{0.02}$, (e) $\dfrac{0.7}{200}$.

2 Find the value of (a) $\dfrac{1 + (0.5)^2}{0.2}$, (b) $\dfrac{1 + (1.5)^2}{0.25}$.

3 Find the value of (a) $\frac{1}{3} + \frac{3}{5}$, (b) $3\frac{1}{3} - 1\frac{3}{5}$.

4 Find the value of (a) $\frac{2}{3}(1\frac{1}{4} + 2\frac{1}{3})$, (b) $\frac{1}{2}\{(1\frac{1}{2})^2 + 1\}$.

5 (a) Express each of the following as a bicimal: 0.25, 0.0625, 0.6.
  (b) Express each of the following bicimals as a decimal: 0.1, 0.01, 0.011.

Standard form

An average adult has about 20 000 000 000 000 red corpuscles in his system; the diameter of a bacterium is 0.000 02 cm. Numbers like these are difficult to write and hard to manipulate, and we usually write them in standard form (sometimes called standard index form), 2×10^{13} and 2×10^{-5}, i.e. in the form $A \times 10^n$, where A is a number between 1 and 10 (including 1 but not 10) and n is an integer, positive or negative. Thus we write

$$2700 = 2.7 \times 10^3 \qquad\qquad 0.27 \quad\; = 2.7 \times 10^{-1}$$
$$270 = 2.7 \times 10^2 \quad\text{and}\quad 0.027 \;\; = 2.7 \times 10^{-2}$$
$$27 = 2.7 \times 10 \qquad\qquad 0.002\,7 = 2.7 \times 10^{-3}.$$

To express a number in standard form, put a decimal marker after the first non-zero digit, then find the correct power of ten, thus

$$27\,000 = 2.7 \times 10\,000 = 2.7 \times 10^4,$$
$$0.000\,27 = 2.7 \times 0.000\,1 = 2.7 \times 10^{-4}.$$

Manipulating numbers in standard form

The powers of ten have to be treated as indices, so that they are added when the numbers are multiplied, and subtracted when the numbers are divided. Thus

$$
\begin{aligned}
&(3 \times 10^4) \times (2 \times 10^5) = 6 \times 10^9\\
&(3 \times 10^4) \times (4 \times 10^5) = 12 \times 10^9 = 1.2 \times 10^{10}
\end{aligned}
$$
and
$$
\begin{aligned}
&(3 \times 10^4) \div (2 \times 10^5) = 1.5 \times 10^{-1}\\
&(3 \times 10^4) \div (4 \times 10^5) = 0.75 \times 10^{-1} = 7.5 \times 10^{-2}
\end{aligned}
$$

Notice that in two of the above examples we did not at first have standard form. We had to write $12 = 1.2 \times 10$ and $0.75 = 7.5 \times 10^{-1}$.

N.B. Take care with negative indices.

Example 1.15 *Carry out the following calculations, leaving each answer in standard form.*

(a) $(4 \times 10^2) \times (7 \times 10^3)$ $= 28 \times 10^5 = 2.8 \times 10^6$
(b) $(4 \times 10^2) \times (7 \times 10^{-4})$ $= 28 \times 10^{-2} = 2.8 \times 10^{-1}$
(c) $(4 \times 10^{-2}) \times (7 \times 10^{-4}) = 28 \times 10^{-6} = 2.8 \times 10^{-5}$
(d) $(7 \times 10^5) \div (4 \times 10^2)$ $= 1.75 \times 10^3$
(e) $(3 \times 10^5) \div (4 \times 10^2)$ $= 0.75 \times 10^3 = 7.5 \times 10^2$
(f) $(3 \times 10^5) \div (4 \times 10^{-2})$ $= 0.75 \times 10^7 = 7.5 \times 10^6$

Exercise 1c

1 Write each of the following numbers in standard form (a) 780, (b) 678 000, (c) 0.008, (d) 0.1.
2 Find the value, in standard form, of (a) $(3 \times 10^2) \times (2 \times 10^3)$, (b) $(3 \times 10^2) \div (2 \times 10^3)$,   (c) $(3 \times 10^2) \div (2 \times 10^{-3})$, (d) $(3 \times 10^{-2}) \div (2 \times 10^{-3})$.
3 Find the value of x/y when (a) $x = 4 \times 10^3$, $y = 2 \times 10^5$, (b) $x = 3 \times 10^4$, $y = 4 \times 10^7$.
4 Arrange in ascending order of size: $0.1, 1.5 \times 10^{-1}, \frac{2}{15}$.

2 Units, area and volume, similarity, accuracy

Notes

Common metric (SI) measures
of length:

    1 km (kilometre) = 1000 m (metres)
    1 m   = 100 cm (centimetres)
                  = 1000 mm (millimetres)

of area:

    1 hectare   = 10 000 m² (square metres)   = 10^4 m²
    1 m²   = 10 000 cm² (square centimetres) = 10^4 cm²

of volume:

    1 m³   = 1 000 000 cm³ (cubic centimetres) = 10^6 cm³
    1 litre   = 1000 cm³

Areas and volumes

The area of a triangle (Fig. 2.1) is $\frac{1}{2}$ base × perpendicular height = $\frac{1}{2} bh$.

The area of a trapezium (Fig. 2.2) is $\frac{1}{2}$ (sum of the parallel sides) × perpendicular distance between them = $\frac{1}{2}(a + b) \times h$.

The circumference of a circle is $2\pi r$; the area of a circle is πr^2.

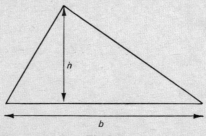

Fig. 2.1

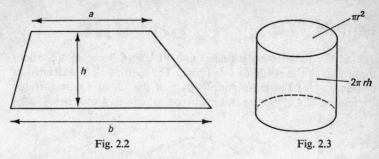

Fig. 2.2   Fig. 2.3

The curved surface area of a cylinder (Fig. 2.3) is $2\pi rh$;
the area of one end is πr^2;
the volume of a cylinder is $\pi r^2 h$.
The curved surface area of a sphere is $4\pi r^2$; the volume of a sphere is $\frac{4}{3}\pi r^3$.
The volume of a cone is $\frac{1}{3}\pi r^2 h$.

Scales and similar figures
If two figures have lengths in the ratio $1:k$, (scale factor, k) corresponding areas are in the ratio $1:k^2$ and corresponding volumes $1:k^3$.
The most useful relations between areas are

$$1\ m^2\ = 1\ 000\ 000\ mm^2\ \text{i.e.}\ (10^6\ mm^2)$$
$$1\ m^2\ =\quad 10\ 000\ cm^2 \quad (10^4\ cm^2)$$
$$1\ km^2 = 1\ 000\ 000\ m^2 \quad (10^6\ m^2)$$

The area of a square 100 m by 100 m is called a hectare, so that

$$1\ \text{hectare (1 ha)} = 10^4\ m^2$$

The area of a full-sized football pitch is just under 1 hectare.

Volume
The unit of volume is the cubic m (m^3), the volume of a cube edge 1 m. As with area, since 1 m $=$ 100 cm, the volume of the cube is also $100 \times 100 \times 100\ cm^3$, so that

$$1\ m^3 = 1\ 000\ 000\ cm^3.$$

The most useful relations between volumes are

$$1\ m^3 = 1\ 000\ 000\ 000\ mm^3\ (10^9\ mm^3)$$
$$1\ m^3 =\quad 1\ 000\ 000\ cm^3\ \ (10^6\ cm^3)$$

1 litre can be taken to be 1000 cm^3.

N.B. Always draw a clear figure to illustrate each question.

Length

The SI (Système Internationale) unit of length is the metre, about the length of the stride of a tall man. The metre was first defined as one-quarter of the ten-millionth part of the Great Circle through Paris (Fig. 2.4); the measurement on which this was based later

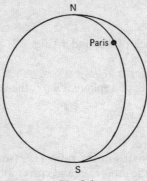

Fig. 2.4

proved inaccurate, and the metre has now been redefined, to the satisfaction of scientists and others, in terms of the wave-length of orange light from krypton

A metre is inconveniently large for some measurements, and too small for others, so that multiples and fractions of the metre are used. The most useful are

$$1 \text{ kilometre (km)} = 1000 \text{ metres (m)}$$
$$100 \text{ centimetres (cm)} = 1 \text{ metre}$$
$$1000 \text{ millimetres (mm)} = 1 \text{ metre}$$

Area

A square, side 2 m, can be divided into four smaller squares, each side 1 m, and we see that the area of the square is 4 square metres (m^2) (Fig. 2.5).

Similarly, a square 1 m by 1 m (with area 1 m^2) can be thought of as a square 100 cm by 100 cm, area 10 000 cm^2, so that

$$1 \text{ m}^2 = 10\,000 \text{ cm}^2$$

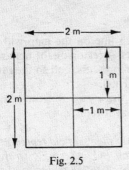

Fig. 2.5

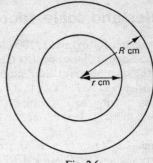

Fig. 2.6

Example 2.1 *A circular washer is bounded by concentric circles, radii R cm and r cm. Find the surface area of one side of the washer if (a) R = 5 and r = 3, (b) R = 5.4 and r = 3.2.*

Draw Fig. 2.6. The surface area A cm² is the difference between two circles, i.e. $\pi R^2 - \pi r^2$.

In (a) $A = \pi \times 5^2 - \pi \times 3^2$; simple numbers like these suggest that a calculator should not be used, so that

$$A = 25\pi - 9\pi$$
$$= 16\pi$$
$$= 50.24 \text{ cm, taking } \pi \text{ to be } 3.14$$

the area is 50.24 cm².

In (b) it will be quicker to use a calculator (or to use logarithms in examinations that do not permit calculators), so

$$A = \pi \times (5.4)^2 - \pi \times (3.2)^2$$
$$\simeq 59.439$$

the area is approximately 59.4 cm².

Areas of similar figures

The areas of similar figures are in the ratio of the squares of their corresponding linear dimensions. If the radius of one circle is twice that of another, their areas are in the ratio 4:1. If the sides of similar triangles are in the ratio 2:3, their areas are in the ratio 4:9. If a model of a railway locomotive is made on a scale 1:20, the surface area of the locomotive is 400 times that of the model.

Scales and scale-factors

If the scale of a map is 1:1000, then each line on the map will be one-thousandth of the line that it represents. A region on the map will be of the same shape as the region that it represents, and so the ratio of the areas will be 1:1000², that is, 1:1 000 000.

When solving scale problems, always draw two diagrams, one showing the scale figure, one the figure that it represents.

Example 2.2 *A map (Fig. 2.7a), scale* 1:5000 *shows a field represented by a rectangle ABCD, with AB = 5 cm and BC = 8 cm. A straight footpath goes from the corner represented by A to the midpoint of the opposite side. Find (a) the length of the footpath, (b) the area of the triangular part of the field, one side of which is the footpath.*

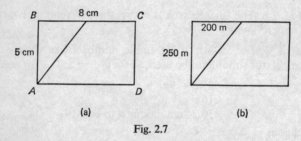

(a)   (b)

Fig. 2.7

Since the scale is 1:5000, 1 cm on the map represents 50 m.

(a) By Pythagoras' theorem, using Fig. 2.7 (b), the length of the footpath is $\sqrt{(200^2 + 250^2)}$, i.e. approximately 320 m.
(b) The area of the triangular region is '½ base × height', $\frac{1}{2} \times 200 \times 250$ m², i.e. 25 000 m².

Volumes of similar solids

Volumes of similar solids are in the ratio of the cubes of their corresponding linear dimensions. If the radius of a sphere is doubled, its volume is increased by a factor of 8. If the heights of two cones are in the ratio 2:3, their volumes are in the ratio 8:27, if the shapes of the cones are the same.

Example 2.3 *A cone height* 10 *cm is cut by a plane parallel to its base,*

4 cm from that base. Find the ratio of (a) the surface areas, (b) the volumes, of the smaller cone to the larger one.

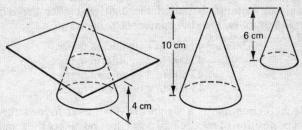

Fig. 2.8

Since the plane is 4 cm from the base, the height of the smaller cone is 6 cm. Since the smaller cone is formed from the larger cone, they are of the same shape, so that

(a) the areas are in the ratio $6^2:10^2$; i.e. $9:25$
(b) the volumes are in the ratio $6^3:10^3$; i.e. $27:125$.

Exercise 2a

These questions should be answered without using a calculator.

1 Find the area of a rectangle, sides (a) 2.4 cm by 7 cm, (b) 3.5 cm by 8 cm.
2 Find the length of a rectangle, given that (a) the area is 40 cm² and the breadth is 2.5 cm, (b) the area is 640 cm² and the breadth is 8 cm.
3 A certain map has a scale of 1 : 50 000.
    (a) What is the length represented by a line 3 cm on the map?
    (b) What length on the map represents a distance of 2 km?
    (c) What is the area of the region represented on the map by a square, area 4 cm².
    (d) What area on the map represents 4 km²?
4 A model, scale factor 1 : 20, is made of a house. Write down the ratio of
    (a) a length of piping in the model to that in the house;
    (b) the area of a window in the model to that in the house;
    (c) the volume of a room in the model to that in the house.

Degree of accuracy: significant figures

The distance between two posts on an airfield may be measured as 2123 m 45 cm, i.e. 2123.45 m. Even this is most unlikely to be exact, and better instruments might give 2123.456, or even more decimal places. For many purposes, 2100 m will be sufficiently accurate, and this degree of accuracy is called 'correct to two significant figures'.

For 'significant figures', start counting at the first non-zero digit; the usual convention† is that if the digit next after the required number is 5 or more, then the number is 'rounded up'.

e.g. $43496 = 40\ 000$ to 1 significant figure,
                    $= 43\ 000$ to 2 significant figures,
                    $= 43\ 500$ to 3 significant figures,
                    $= 43\ 500$ to 4 significant figures,

the first zero counting as a significant digit, as it follows the non-zero 5. The position of the decimal point does not affect the significant figures,

e.g. $0.045036 = 0.05$ to 1 significant figure,
                    $= 0.045$ to 2 significant figures,
                    $= 0.0450$ to 3 significant figures,
                                zeros only counting when they follow non-zero digits.

Decimal places

In some calculations we require results 'correct to a certain number of decimal places', which means that we start counting at the decimal point, however many digits are to the left of that decimal point.

Thus 435.678 $= 435.68$ to 2 decimal places,
            $4.35678 =$ 4.36 to 2 decimal places,
            $0.04356 =$ 0.04 to 2 decimal places.

Estimates of calculations

It is most important that we always carry out a rough check of our calculations, and to do this we shall want to make a suitable approximation to the numbers in a calculation. Often 1 significant figure is appropriate.

Example 2.4 *Correct each number to* 1 *significant figure, and so estimate the value of* $\dfrac{0.43 \times 5.7}{0.078}$

---

† There are other conventions, such as correcting to the nearest even number – or the nearest odd number! Ignore them at present.

Correcting each number to 1 significant figure,

$$\frac{0.43 \times 5.7}{0.078} = \frac{0.4 \times 6}{0.08}$$

$$= \frac{240}{8}$$

$$= 30$$

Exercise 2b

1 Correct each of the following to two significant figures
5321; 5371; 5351; 0.5321; 0.5032; 0.5003.

2 Correct each of the following to two decimal places
5.352; 5.357; 5.355; 5.350; 0.5503; 0.5553; 0.5053; 0.5005.

3 Correct each number to 1 significant figure, and so estimate the value of
(a) $\pi \times (4.3)^2$ (b) $\pi \times 4.3 \times 5.7$

(c) $\dfrac{\pi}{\sqrt{124}}$ (d) $\dfrac{(9.87)^2}{6.4 + (2.1)^2}$

3 Ratio and percentage, tax, and interest

Notes

Percentage is merely a fraction with denominator 100,

e.g. $$17\% = \frac{17}{100}$$

Percentage **error** $= \dfrac{\text{error}}{\text{correct measurement}} \times 100$

Percentage **profit** $= \dfrac{\text{profit}}{\text{price for which it was bought by the seller}} \times 100 = \dfrac{\text{profit}}{\text{outlay}} \times 100$

Simple interest I on a loan (principal) P for T years at $R\%$ per annum (p.a.) is given by

$$I = \frac{P\,R\,T}{100}$$

Compound interest is $A - P$, where A is the amount and

$$A = P\left(1 + \frac{R}{100}\right)^{T}$$

N.B. Remember to subtract the principal P.

Ratio

A map may be drawn to a scale $1:5000$. This means that 1 cm on the map represents a distance of 5000 cm. A magnum of champagne is twice the volume of an ordinary bottle; their volumes are in the ratio $2:1$. Two quantities of the same kind can always be compared in this manner.

Example 3.1 (*a*) *A man is 45 years old, his son is 15 years old. Their* *ages are in the ratio* 3:1 (*b*) *The speed of a cyclist is* 15 *km/h, the speed of a car is* 75 *km/h. The ratio of their speeds is* 1:5 (*c*) *The price of a television licence was* £5; *it is now* £15. *The ratio of the old price to the new is* 1:3.

It is always important that the order of the numbers is the same as the order of the items being compared. In (*c*), the ratio of the old price to the new is 1:3, the ratio of the new price to the old is 3:1.

Example 3.2 *The sides of a triangle are in the ratio* 2:3:4. *The perimeter is* 18 *cm. Find the length of each side.*

Since the sides are in the ratio 2:3:4, we must divide the perimeter into 9 parts, each 2 cm long. Then the smallest side will have length two parts, i.e. 4 cm. Similarly the next side will have length 3 parts, and the largest side 4 parts. The lengths are 4 cm, 6 cm, and 8 cm.

Exercise 3a

1 Three men form a syndicate for gambling. Their stakes one week are £4.50, £3.60, £1.80. Express these as a ratio in its simplest terms.
2 *A* is twice as old as *B*, who is three times as old as *C*. Find the ratio of their ages.
3 Ann earns half as much as Beth; Beth earns three times as much as Chris. Find the ratio of their earnings.
4 Divide £5 between three friends in the ratio 2:3:5.
5 Three men invested £2000, £3000, and £4000 in a business. The profit each receives is proportional to the money invested. How much does each receive when the total profits are £4500?
6 A sum of money is divided between three men *X*, *Y*, and *Z* in the ratio 2:3:5. If *Y* receives £2.40 less than *Z*, how much does each receive?

Percentages

Suppose that in a certain box of 50 eggs, 7 are bad. Then we can say that the ratio of the number of bad eggs to the total number of eggs is 7:50, which is equal to 14:100. A ratio in which the second term is 100 can be put as a percentage, here 14 per cent (or 14%). We see that

14% is equivalent to the ratio 14:100 or 7:50;

14% is equivalent to the fraction $\frac{14}{100}$;

14% is equivalent to the decimal 0.14.

Some of the simpler percentages can easily be expressed as fractions,

$$75\% \text{ is } \tfrac{3}{4}$$
$$66\tfrac{2}{3}\% \text{ is } \tfrac{2}{3}$$
$$50\% \text{ is } \tfrac{1}{2}$$
$$33\tfrac{1}{3}\% \text{ is } \tfrac{1}{3}$$
and
$$25\% \text{ is } \tfrac{1}{4}$$

To express one quantity as a percentage of another, first write it as a fraction of the second quantity, then multiply by 100.

Example 3.3 *One Saturday Everton scored* 7 *of the* 35 *goals scored in the First division. What percentage was this of the goals scored?*

The percentage of the goals scored by Everton was

$$\tfrac{7}{35} \times 100, \text{ i.e. } 20\%$$

Example 3.4 *The length of a rectangle is increased by* 20% *and the breadth decreased by* 20%. *Find the percentage change in area.*

If the length of the rectangle was l units, a 20% increase is $\tfrac{20}{100}\,l$, and so the new length is $\tfrac{120}{100}\,l$ units. Similarly, if the breadth was b units, the new breadth is $\tfrac{80}{100}\,b$ units. The area was lb square units, and now is $\tfrac{120}{100}\,l \times \tfrac{80}{100}\,b$, i.e. $\tfrac{96}{100}\,lb$ square units, so that the new area as a percentage of the old is

$$\frac{\tfrac{96}{100}\,lb}{lb} \times 100,$$

i.e. 96%, a decrease of 4%.

Percentage profit and loss

If a dealer buys an article for £5 and sells it for £6 his profit is £1; this is one-fifth, i.e. 20% of his outlay. Similarly, if he buys an article for £10 and sells it for £6 his loss, £4, is 40% of his outlay. In schools we always calculate the percentage profit or loss as a percentage of the outlay (*cost price*); commercial practice is different, shopkeepers finding it convenient to express their profit or loss as a percentage of their receipts (*selling price*).

If a trader sells an article at 20% profit, the selling price is 120% of the cost price; if he sells it at 20% loss, the selling price is 80% of the cost price. More generally, when selling at $x\%$ profit,

$$\text{selling price} = \frac{100 + x}{100} \text{ cost price,}$$

$$\text{cost price} = \frac{100}{100 + x} \text{ selling price.}$$

When selling at $x\%$ loss,

$$\text{selling price} = \frac{100 - x}{100} \text{ cost price,}$$

$$\text{cost price} = \frac{100}{100 - x} \text{ selling price.}$$

For practice, copy and complete the table below:

Cost price (outlay)	% profit (or loss)	Multiplying factor	Profit or loss	Selling price
£60	40%	$\frac{140}{100}$		
£80			£20	
			£25	£75
	60%	$\frac{100}{160}$		£80
	30%		£15	
£60				£75

Although profit and loss are the simplest percentage changes made in a quantity, many other changes can be expressed as percentages of the original quantity. The extension in a bar when heated may be a percentage of the unheated length of the bar; the change in volume when chemicals are mixed may be a percentage of the total volume of the chemicals being mixed. The error in a faulty speedometer may indicate a speed a certain percentage more (or less) than the correct speed.

Example 3.5 *The population of a certain town increases each year by 10% of the population at the beginning of that year. The population at the beginning of 1978 was 66 000. Calculate the population (a) at the beginning of 1977 (b) at the beginning of 1979.*

(a) The population in 1978 is 10% more than the population in 1977, i.e. the population in 1978 is 110% of the population in 1977. As the population in 1978 is 66 000, the population in 1977 was

$$\frac{100}{110} \times 66\,000, \text{ i.e. } 60\,000$$

(b) The population in 1979 is 110% of the population in 1978, so the population in 1979 is

$$\frac{110}{100} \times 66\,000, \text{ i.e. } 72\,600$$

Thus the population was 60 000 in 1977 and 72 600 in 1979.

Value added tax and income tax

Many taxes are expressed as a certain percentage of the quantity taxed. At present, there is value-added tax on many items, e.g. if the hairdresser's price for styling is £5, VAT of 75p (15% of £5) is added, so that the customer has to pay £5.75.

Income tax is usually levied as a certain percentage of a person's taxable income within given limits. Thus a man may pay income tax at 25% of the first £750 of taxable income, then 33% of the remainder. The rates of tax in Great Britain are fixed each year (or as occasion requires) in a Budget presented to Parliament.

Example 3.6 *A man has a taxable income of* £2500. *Tax is levied at* 25% *on the first* £750, *and* 33% *on the remainder. Find the tax he pays.*

On the first £750, he pays   £187.50.
On the remaining £1750 he pays £577.50.
The total tax paid by the man is £765.00.

Exercise 3b

1 Calculate 40% of 320.
2 40% of a certain number is 320. What was the original number?
3 When a girl's salary has been increased by 40% it is £4200. What was her salary before the increase?
4 A salesman receives commission of 4% of the value of the goods he sells. Calculate (a) his commission when he sells goods value £48, (b) the value of the goods he sold when he received £19.20 commission.
5 If x litres of antifreeze is poured into y litres of water, what percentage of the final mixture is water?
6 The VAT on a new lawnmower is £2.56, VAT being 8% of the original price. What was the original price of the lawnmower, and how much did the purchaser have to pay for the lawnmower?

7 Only 64% of the voters in a constituency of 45 000 actually voted.
   Of the votes cast, candidate A received 40%, candidate B received 22%,
   and candidate C the remainder. How many votes did C receive?
8 In a school of 700 boys, every boy plays football or hockey or both.
   74% play football and 66% play hockey. How many boys play both?
9 One year the taxable income of a certain man was £7600. He paid
   tax at 33% on the first £5000, 43% on the next £1000, and 50% on
   the remainder. How much tax did he pay that year?
10 In the same year, his friend had a taxable income of £5850. How much
   tax did he have to pay?

Simple interest

When money is saved and invested, the investor receives some *interest*
each year, which is often a fixed percentage of the money invested
(the *principal*). If the interest agreed is 5%, then for an investment of
£400, the saver would have received £20 per year (p.a. for per
annum). If the money was invested for 5 years, he would receive
£20 each year, a total of £100.

If £P is invested for T years at R per cent per annum, then the
interest £I is given by

$$I = \frac{PRT}{100}$$

This formula can be transposed to give

$$T = \frac{100\,I}{PR}, \ R = \frac{100\,I}{PT}, \ \text{and} \ P = \frac{100\,I}{RT}$$

if we know the interest earned and wish to find one of the other quantities.

Example 3.7 *Find the* (*simple*) *interest on a loan of* £480 *for* 4 *years
at* $7\frac{1}{2}$% *p.a.*

Write the $7\frac{1}{2}$ as $\frac{15}{2}$. Then the interest in £ is

$$\frac{480 \times 4 \times 15}{100 \times 2} \text{ i.e. £144.00}$$

Compound interest

If, instead of drawing the interest each year, we leave it to increase
the value of the savings, then we have more and more money in-

vested each year, and so more and more interest is earned each year. This is cal'ed compound interest.

If £200 is invested at 8% p.a. compound interest, we can set out the calculations to find the value of the investment after three years like this.

Principal initially	£200.00
Interest for 1st year, 8% of £200	16.00
Principal for 2nd year	216.00
Interest for 2nd year, 8% of £216	17.28
Principal for 3rd year	233.28
Interest for 3rd year, 8% of £233.28	18.66 (correct to the nearest penny)
Amount after three years	£251.94

Working the same problem algebraically, with principal £P invested at R% p.a. for T years, the amount £A is given by the formula

$$A = P\left(1 + \frac{R}{100}\right)^T$$

Using this formula in the example gives

$$A = 200\,(1.08)^3$$
$$= 251.94, \text{ correct to two decimal places}$$

The amount invested is £251.94; the interest that has been earned is £51.94.

To find the interest, remember to subtract the principal from the amount.

Exercise 3c

1 Find the simple interest on £680 for 5 years at 5% p.a.

2 Find the simple interest on £48 for $2\frac{1}{2}$ years at $7\frac{1}{2}$% p.a.

3 Find the simple interest on £640 for 5 months at 6% p.a.

4 Find the simple interest, correct to the nearest £, on
   (a) £860 for $5\frac{1}{2}$ years at $8\frac{1}{2}$% p.a.
   (b) £57.40 for 12 years at 5% p.a.
   (c) £360 for 2 years 8 months at 8% p.a.

5 If the simple interest on £280 borrowed for 4 years is £39.20, at what rate per cent per annum has interest been charged?

6 If the simple interest on a loan of £2200 at 8% is £44, for how long has the money been borrowed?

7 If the simple interest on a loan at 3% p.a. for $2\frac{1}{2}$ years is £120, how much money was borrowed?

8 A loan of £120 was completely discharged after two years by a payment of £134.40, i.e. £134.40 repaid the principal and the interest due. At what rate per cent per annum was interest charged?

9 A loan of £250 was completely discharged by a payment of £375 after 4 years. At what rate per cent per annum had the interest been charged?

10 A man borrowed £5000 on 1 January 1974. He undertook to repay £1000 on 1 January 1975 and each succeeding year until the debt was repaid. Interest at 8% of the amount outstanding each year was added at the end of each year. How much was owing at the end of 1974, 1975, 1976, and 1977?

11 A man invested £500 on 1 January 1977, £1000 on 1 January 1978, and £500 on 1 January 1979. Interest at 8% of the amount to his credit was added at the end of each year. If the man did not make any withdrawals, how much had he to his credit at the end of 1979, when interest for that year had been added?

12 Find the compound interest on a loan of
  (a) £600 for 4 years at 5% p.a.;
  (b) £400 for 3 years at 8% p.a.;
  (c) £800 for 10 years at 10% p.a.;
  (d) £1000 for 14 years at 5% p.a.

4 Algebra: factors

Notes on Algebra

Factors

$$ab + ac = a(b + c)$$
$$a^2 - b^2 = (a - b)(a + b)$$
$$a^2 - 2ab + b^2 = (a - b)(a - b)$$
$$a^2 + 2ab + b^2 = (a + b)(a + b)$$
$$a^2 + b^2 \text{ has no factors}$$

Indices

$$a^m \times a^n = a^{m+n}, \text{e.g. } a^2 \times a^3 = a^5$$
$$a^m \div a^n = a^{m-n}, \text{e.g. } a^6 \div a^2 = a^4$$
$$(a^m)^n = a^{mn}$$
$$a^0 = 1$$
$$a^{-m} = \frac{1}{a^m}$$
$$a^{p/q} = \sqrt[q]{a^p}$$

Solution of quadratic equations

If a quadratic equation factorizes as $(x - a)(x + b) = 0$, the roots are $x = a$ or $-b$. *Note the change of signs.*

If the quadratic equation $ax^2 + bx + c = 0$ does not factorize easily, use the formula

$$x = \frac{-b \pm \sqrt{b^2 - 4ac}}{2a}$$

Inequalities

If
$$(x - a)(x - b) < 0 \text{ and } a < b,$$
$$a < x < b$$

If
$$(x - a)(x - b) > 0 \text{ and } a < b$$
$$x < a \text{ or } b < x$$

Logarithms

$$\log a + \log b = \log ab$$
$$\log a - \log b = \log (a/b)$$
$$n \log a = \log (a^n)$$
$$\log_b a = \frac{\log_x a}{\log_x b}$$

Progressions

In an **arithmetic** progression, the **difference** between each pair of consecutive terms is constant.

The nth term of an arithmetic progression is $a + (n - 1)d$. The sum of the first n terms is $\frac{n}{2} \{2a + (n - 1)d\}$ or $\frac{n}{2} (a + l)$.

In a **geometric** progression, the **ratio** of each pair of consecutive terms is constant. The nth term of a geometric progression is ar^{n-1}; the sum of the first n terms is $a \dfrac{r^n - 1}{r - 1}$.

Common or 'shouting' factor

Two or more terms may have a factor in common, e.g.

$$xy + xz = x(y + z)$$
$$3a + 12b = 3(a + 4b)$$
$$6ab + 15bc = 3b(2a + 5c)$$
$$x^2y + xy^2 + xyz = xy(x + y + z)$$

Example 4.1 *Factorize* $12x^2y - 9x^3 + 3x^2$.

Notice first that each coefficient contains a factor 3, so that

$$12x^2y - 9x^3 + 3x^2 = 3(4x^2y - 3x^3 + x^2)$$

The terms inside the bracket have highest common factor x^2 (notice x^2, not just x), so that

$$12x^2y - 9x^3 + 3x^2 = 3x^2(4y - 3x + 1)$$

Exercise 4a

Factorize:

1 $4x - 6xy$	**2** $4h^2 - 6h$	**3** $4y - 12y^2$
4 $x^2 + 3x^3$	**5** $x^2 + x^5$	**6** $x^2 + x^6$
7 $2a^2 + 6a^3 - 4a^2b$	**8** $3x^2y + 3x^2$	
9 $a^4 + a^3 + a^2$	**10** $4x^2 + 8x^3 + 12x^4 + 16x^5$	

Difference of two squares

Since $(x - y)(x + y) = x^2 - y^2$, by multiplication, we can deduce that $x^2 - y^2 = (x - y)(x + y)$, so that every expression that is the difference of two squares can be factorized,

e.g. $\qquad a^2 - b^2 = (a - b)(a + b)$

We may need to write one (or both) terms as a perfect square,

e.g. $\qquad\qquad 4x^2 - y^2 = (2x)^2 - y^2$
$$= (2x - y)(2x + y)$$
and $\qquad\qquad 4x^2 - 9y^2 = (2x)^2 - (3y)^2$
$$= (2x - 3y)(2x + 3y)$$

or we may need to find a common factor first,

e.g. $\qquad\qquad x^2y - yz^2 = y(x^2 - z^2)$
$$= y(x - z)(x + z)$$

and with the occasional harder factor, the brackets may not even consist only of one term,

e.g. $\qquad x^2 - (y - z)^2 = \{x - (y - z)\}\{x + (y - z)\}$
$$= \{x - y + z\}\{x + y - z\}$$

Example 4.2

(a) $2x^2 - 18y^2 = 2(x^2 - 9y^2)$
$$= 2(x^2 - (3y)^2)$$
$$= 2(x - 3y)(x + 3y)$$

(b) $\pi R^2h - \pi r^2h = \pi h(R^2 - r^2)$
$$= \pi h(R - r)(R + r)$$

(c) $\qquad 1 - 16z^2 = 1 - (4z)^2$
$$= (1 - 4z)(1 + 4z)$$

Exercise 4b

Factorize:

1 $x^2 - y^2$ $\qquad$ **2** $p^2 - 49q^2$ $\qquad$ **3** $25a^2 - 9b^2$
4 $2s^2 - 18t^2$ $\qquad$ **5** $4 - 36x^2$ $\qquad$ **6** $7y - 63y^3$
7 $a^2b - c^2b$ $\qquad$ **8** $x^4 - 1$ $\qquad$ **9** $a^2 - (b - c)^2$
10 $\pi(x - y)^2 - \pi z^2$

Simplify without using tables or calculators:

11 $5.11^2 - 4.89^2$ $\qquad\qquad$ **12** $5.1^2 - 4.9^2$
13 $1001^2 - 999^2$ $\qquad\qquad$ **14** $3.14 \times 5.77 + 3.14 \times 4.23$

Trinomials

Multiplying, we see that $(x + 3)(x + 4) = x(x + 4) + 3(x + 4)$
$$= x^2 + 4x + 3x + 12$$
$$= x^2 + 7x + 12$$

12 is the product of $+3$ and $+4$, 7 is the sum of $+3$ and $+4$.

If we need to factorize $x^2 + 9x + 20$, we have to find two numbers whose product is 20 and whose sum is 9. We may find $+4$ and $+5$, by trial and error. When the coefficient of x^2 is 1, trial and error is usually the simplest method.

Example 4.3 *Factorize* $x^2 + 7x + 10$.

Look for two numbers whose product is 10 and whose sum is 7. Always start by finding the pairs of factors of the product. The factors of 10 are $+1$ and $+10$, $+2$ and $+5$, -1 and -10, -2 and -5. The pair whose sum is 7 is $+2$ and $+5$, so that

$$x^2 + 7x + 10 = (x + 2)(x + 5).$$

Example 4.4 *Factorize* $x^2 - 3x - 10$.

Now we require two numbers whose product is -10 and whose sum is -3. Possible pairs of factors are -1 and $+10$, -2 and $+5$, -5 and $+2$, -10 and $+1$. The pair whose sum is -3 is $+2$ and -5, so that

$$x^2 - 3x - 10 = (x + 2)(x - 5).$$

When the constant term is 1, we can proceed to find numbers whose product is the coefficient of x^2, and whose sum is the coefficient of x.

Example 4.5 *Factorize* $8x^2 + 6x + 1$.

The factors of 8 are 1 and 8, 2 and 4, -1 and -8, and -2 and -4. The pair whose sum is 6 is $+2$ and $+4$, so that

$$8x^2 + 6x + 1 = (4x + 1)(2x + 1)$$

When neither the coefficient of x^2 nor the constant term is 1, trial and error is sometimes shortened by the following method.

Example 4.6 *Factorize* $6x^2 + 11x - 10$.

Try pairs of factors of 6 and of -10, setting out the working as below.

$$\begin{vmatrix} 6 & 5 \\ 1 & -2 \end{vmatrix}$$
$$-12 + 5 = -7$$

$$\begin{vmatrix} 3 & 5 \\ 2 & -2 \end{vmatrix}$$
$$-6 + 10 = 4$$

$$\begin{vmatrix} 3 & -2 \\ 2 & 5 \end{vmatrix}$$
$$15 - 4 = 11$$

Crossmultiply the numbers and add the products; look for an arrangement in which the sum of the products is equal to the coefficient of x. The third arrangement satisfies these conditions, so the factors are $(3x - 2)(2x + 5)$.

Exercise 4c

Factorize:

1 $x^2 + 7x + 6$ 2 $x^2 - 5x + 6$ 3 $y^2 - y - 6$
4 $z^2 - 5z - 6$ 5 $x^2 - 4x - 12$ 6 $4x^2 - 3x - 1$
7 $3x^2 - x - 2$ 8 $3y^2 - 7y - 6$ 9 $5 + 6y + y^2$
10 $4x^2 - 2x - 30$

Grouping factors

When an expression contains four terms, group in pairs so that each pair has a common factor,

e.g. $ax + ay - bx - by = a(x + y) - b(x + y)$

$(x + y)$ is a common factor, so that

$$a(x + y) - b(x + y) = (x + y)(a - b)$$

Always write the common factor, here $(x + y)$, first.

Example 4.7 *Factorize* $4x - 4y + ay - ax$

$$4x - 4y + ay - ax = 4(x - y) + a(y - x)$$

Remember that $(y - x) = -(x - y)$, so that

$$4x - 4y + ay - ax = 4(x - y) - a(x - y)$$
$$= (x - y)(4 - a).$$

Example 4.8 *Factorize* $a^2 + 2ab + b^2 + a + b$.

For hard factors like this, look for the trinomial first.

$$a^2 + 2ab + b^2 + a + b = (a + b)^2 + (a + b)$$
$$= (a + b)(a + b + 1)$$

Exercise 4d

Factorize:

1 $a^2 + 2a + ax + 2x$ 2 $xy + 4x + 2y + 8$
3 $x^2 + 2x + xy + 2y$ 4 $xy - xz - y^2 + yz$
5 $x^2 - y^2 + x + y$ 6 $x^2 - y^2 + x - y$
7 $z^2 + 3z + 2 + az + 2a$ 8 $y^2 + 7y + yx + 10 + 5x$

Exercise 4e : Miscellaneous factors

Factorize:

1 $a^2c - b^2c$ 2 $a^2c - bc$
3 $a^2c - abc$ 4 $ab + ac + b^2 + bc$
5 $4a^2 - 3a - 1$ 6 $15 + 7t - 4t^2$
7 $2ax - 3ay - 2bx + 3by$ 8 $18x^2 - 50y^2$
9 $x^2 + 4x + 4 + 10xy + 20y$ 10 $a^3bc - abc$

5 Algebra: equations and inequalities

Constructing equations

If we buy 6 buns for 5 pence each, the cost is 30p. If we buy x buns at q pence each, the cost is xq pence. Suppose now we buy 6 buns for 5 pence each, and 4 cakes at 7 pence each, the total cost is 30p + 28p, i.e. 58 pence. We had to note clearly the meaning of each of these numbers to see which to add and which to multiply.

Suppose that a cake always costs 2 pence more than a bun. Then if the cost of a bun is x pence, the cost of a cake is $(x + 2)$ pence, 2 pence more, $x + 2$. If we buy 5 buns, the cost of the buns is $5x$ pence. If we buy 8 cakes, the cost of the cakes is $8(x + 2)$ pence. The total cost of these purchases is $5x + 8(x + 2)$ pence. (Notice that we have written pence in full, and not used the abbreviation p – this can be confused with the unknowns in algebra problems.) If the total cost of these purchases is 94 pence, then we have the equation

$$5x + 8(x + 2) = 94$$

Expressions

We found that the total cost of the purchases was $5x + 8(x + 2)$ pence. This is an **expression**, which can be simplified but not solved. Here $5x + 8(x + 2) = 13x + 16$, a simpler form for the total cost of the purchase.

Travel problems

Many problems that occur are concerned with travelling. If in doubt about the relation of distance, speed, and time, always make up simple numerical questions.

Example 5.1 *A man walks for 3 hours at x km/h and then cycles for 2 hours at $(x + 5)$ km/h. How far has he travelled?*

If he walks for 3 hours at 6 km/h, he will travel 18 km, so if he walks for 3 hours at x km/h, he travels $3x$ km. Similarly, cycling at $(x + 5)$ km/h for 2 hours, he travels $2(x + 5)$ km. Thus the total distance he travels is $3x + 2(x + 5)$, i.e. $5x + 10$ km.

If we know the numerical value of the expression, as when the food cost 94 pence, we can solve the resulting equation.

When solving equations, always think what algebraic operation, like adding, subtracting, multiplying, or dividing, we are doing, and make sure that we carry out the same operation on both sides of the equation. It often helps to write down what we are doing at each stage.

Example 5.2 *A certain hotel charges £x a day for an adult and £5 less a day for a child. A family of two adults and three children stay there for 6 days and the bill is £510. How much does the hotel charge per day for an adult?*

Since the daily charge for a child is £5 less than the charge for an adult, the charge for a child is $£(x − 5)$. The daily charge for the two adults is $£2x$, so their bill for 6 days is $£12x$. The daily charge for the three children is $£3 (x − 5)$, so their bill for 6 days is $£18 (x − 5)$. Since the total bill is £510,

$$12x + 18(x − 5) = 510$$
i.e. $$12x + 18x − 90 = 510$$
$$30x − 90 = 510$$
Adding 90 to both sides $$30x = 600$$
Dividing both sides by 30 $$x = 20$$

The daily charge for an adult is £20.

Exercise 5a

1 A pencil costs 2 pence more than a biro. A man buys 10 biros at x pence each, and 12 pencils. He spends £1.78 on these items. Form an equation and solve it to find the cost of a biro.

2 Railway excursion tickets for a certain journey cost £5 for an adult and £3 for a child. A party of football supporters contains five times as many adults as children; their tickets cost a total of £252.

(a) If there are x children in the party, how many adults are there?
(b) Form an equation and solve it to find x.

3 Tickets for a school concert cost either 30p or 50p each. One hundred more of the cheaper tickets were sold than the dearer. If x was the number of 50p tickets sold, write down an expression for the total receipts, in pence, from the concert. If the total receipts were £74, form an equation in x and solve it to find how many of each price of tickets were sold.

4 A girl rides x km at 10 km/h, then walks half as far at 3 km/h. If the whole journey takes 4 hours, form an equation and solve it to find how far she rides.

5 A motorist drives x km at 80 km/h then $(x + 10)$ km in 4 hours. His average speed for the whole of the journey was 70 km/h. Find the length of the whole journey.

Harder linear equations

Equations in which the only unknown is x^1 (written just x, of course) are called *linear* equations. The equations in Exercise 5a were fairly easy. The principle, carrying out the same operation to both sides of the equation, holds for all equations, however difficult they may be.

Example 5.3 *Solve for* x $\dfrac{x + 1}{3} - \dfrac{x - 2}{4} = 0$

Points to watch

1 The minus sign in front of the second term applies to every term obtained from that fraction.

2 Do not forget when we multiply the right-hand side (R.H.S.) by 12, that $12 \times 0 = 0$. Even when the R.H.S. is not zero, it is easy to forget to multiply it by the same term as the L.H.S.

Solution

Multiply both sides of the equation by the L.C.M. of the denominators, i.e. 12.

$$\frac{12(x + 1)}{3} - \frac{12(x - 2)}{4} = 0$$

i.e.
$$4(x + 1) - 3(x - 2) = 0$$
$$4x + 4 - 3x + 6 = 0$$
$$x + 10 = 0$$

Subtracting 10 from both sides $x = -10$

Check this solution by seeing if it satisfies the original equation.

$$\frac{-10 + 1}{3} - \frac{-10 - 2}{4} = -3 + 3 = 0$$

as expected.

Exercise 5b

Solve for x.

1 $5x = 4$

2 $5x - 3 = 4$

3 $\dfrac{x}{3} - \dfrac{x-1}{2} = 0$

4 $\dfrac{x}{3} - \dfrac{x-1}{2} = 1$

5 $\dfrac{x}{3} - 2(x-3) = 0$

6 $\dfrac{x}{3} - 2(x-3) = 1$

7 $\dfrac{x}{3} - \dfrac{3-x}{2} = x$

8 $\dfrac{x}{4} - \dfrac{3-x}{8} = 3$

9 If $ax = 4$ has a solution $x = \frac{1}{2}$, find the value of a.

10 If $ax + b = 1$ has a solution $x = 2$, and b is known to be -1, find a.

Inequalities

Linear inequalities are solved in the same way as linear equations, except that we have to take care that, whenever possible, we multiply or divide by positive numbers. For, although if $x > 2$, then $2x > 4$, it is also true that $-x < -2$. To verify this, $x = 3$ is one value that satisfies the original inequality, but we see that $-x = -3$, which is less than -2.

Example 5.4 *Find the range of values of x if* $4x - 3 < 5$.

Notice that for an inequality we usually have a range of values of x, not just one value.

If $\qquad\qquad\qquad 4x - 3 < 5,$

adding 3 to both sides, $\qquad 4x < 8$

dividing both sides by 4, $\qquad x < 2.$

Example 5.5 *Find the range of values of x if* $3 - 4x < 5$.

If $\qquad\qquad\qquad 3 - 4x < 5$

subtracting 3 from both sides, $-4x < 2$

We can now divide both sides by -4, if we remember to change the inequality,

$$x > -\tfrac{1}{2}$$

But it may be wiser to add $4x$ to both sides,

$$0 < 2 + 4x$$

then subtract 2 from both sides $-2 < 4x$

finally divide both sides by $+4$, $-\tfrac{1}{2} < x.$

Check   An easy value of x which satisfies $x > -\frac{1}{2}$ is $x = 0$. Substituting this in the original inequality, $3 - 4(0) = 3$, which is less than 5.

Exercise 5c

Find the range of values of x satisfying the following inequalities.

1 $3x - 4 < 2$

2 $3x + 4 < 2$

3 $4 - 3x < 2$

4 $4 - 3x < -2$

5 $2x - 3(x - 1) < 10$

6 $2x - 3(x - 1) < 5$

7 $\dfrac{x}{2} - \dfrac{2(x-1)}{3} < 1$

8 $\dfrac{x}{2} - \dfrac{2(x-1)}{3} < 0$

Form inequalities and solve them to find the range of values of x satisfying the following sets of data.

9 A boy scored $x\%$ in the first of two exams, and 8% more in the second exam, each paper being marked out of 100. His average mark was over 60%.

10 A boy bought x 10-pence stamps, and $(x + 5)$ 7-pence stamps. He spent less than £5.

Simultaneous equations

Sometimes it is easier to have two unknowns when trying to form equations from given information and to try to obtain two equations. The equations may be of the type in this example.

Example 5.6 *Solve for x and y*, $3x + 4y = 1$ \hfill (1)

$$2x - 3y = 2 \tag{2}$$

Multiply (1) by 3, $\qquad 9x + 12y = 3$ \hfill (3)

Multiply (2) by 4, $\qquad 8x - 12y = 8$ \hfill (4)

Add (3) and (4) so that the terms containing y vanish,

$$17x = 11$$

i.e. $\qquad\qquad x = \dfrac{11}{17}$

Substitute in (1) $\qquad 3\left(\dfrac{11}{17}\right) + 4y = 1$

$$4y = 1 - \dfrac{33}{17}$$

$$= -\dfrac{16}{17}$$

$$y = \dfrac{-4}{17}$$

Check in (2)

$$2\left(\frac{11}{17}\right) - 3\left(\frac{-4}{17}\right) = \frac{22}{17} + \frac{12}{17} = 2$$

N.B.

1 As addition is slightly easier than subtraction, multiply the equations by suitable numbers so that the coefficients of y are equal and opposite, here 12 and -12.

2 Substitute in the equation in which the coefficient of y is positive, here equation (1).

Example 5.7 *The sum of the ages of a father and his daughter is 43 years. Four years ago, the father was six times as old as his daughter. Find their present ages.*

Let the father's present age be x years and the daughter's present age be y years.

Then $\qquad\qquad\qquad x + y = 43$

Four years ago, the father's age was $(x - 4)$ years, and the daughter's age was $(y - 4)$ years, so that

$$x - 4 = 6(y - 4)$$
i.e. $\qquad\qquad x - 4 = 6y - 24$
$$x - 6y = -20$$

The equations to solve are

$$x + y = 43 \qquad\qquad (1)$$
$$x - 6y = -20 \qquad\qquad (2)$$

Subtract (2) from (1), taking care with the negative terms.

$$7y = 63$$
$\therefore \qquad\qquad\qquad y = 9$

Substituting in (1), $\qquad x = 34$

so the father's present age is 34 years, and his daughter's age is 9 years.

Exercise 5d

1 Solve the simultaneous equations $5x + 3y = 7$
$$x - 2y = 1$$
2 Solve the simultaneous equations $5x + 3y = 7$
$$y - 2x = 1$$

3 By factorizing the second equation, solve for x and y

$$x - 2y = 3$$
$$x^2 - 4y^2 = 18$$

4 The equation of a straight line can be written in the form $y = ax + b$. Find the equation of the straight line that passes through the points $(1, -1)$ and $(2, 2)$.

5 At a concert the prices of the seats were 20p and 40p; programmes were 5p each. Half of those buying 40p seats bought programmes, but only one-fifth of those in 20p seats did so. The receipts from the sale of seats were £56; from the sale of programmes were £3.20. How many of each price of seats were sold?

Identities

The equation $x + 3 = 5$ is only satisfied by one value of x, $x = 2$. But an equation like $2(x + 3) = 2x + 6$ is satisfied by all values of x; such an equation is called an **identity.** All equations that we write when factorizing expressions are identities, for they are satisfied by all values of the unknowns. We usually denote an identity by $\equiv$, so perhaps we ought to write

$$x^2 - 4 \equiv (x - 2)(x + 2)$$

but we usually only write $\equiv$ when we wish to emphasize that we are considering an identity and not just an equation.

If two expressions are identically equal, then they must have the same coefficients of the corresponding powers of x on each side of the identity, i.e. if $ax^2 + bx + c \equiv 3x^2 + 2x + 7$, then $a = 3$, $b = 2$, and $c = 7$.

Example 5.8 *Find the constants A, B, and C if $Ax(x - 1) + B(x - 1) + Cx = 2x^2 - 3x - 3$.*

Method 1
The L.H.S. can be written $Ax^2 - Ax + Bx - B + Cx$,
so that $Ax^2 + (-A + B + C)x - B = 2x^2 - 3x - 3$
Equating coefficients of x^2

$$A = 2$$

Equating coefficients of x

$$-A + B + C = -3 \tag{1}$$

Equating constant terms

$$-B = -3$$

Substituting $A = 2$ and $B = 3$ in (1), $C = -4$
So $A = 2$, $B = 3$, and $C = -4$

Method 2

Since this is an identity, it is true for all values of x.

When $x = 0$,

$$A \times 0 + B(-1) + C \times 0 = -3$$
$$\text{so } B = \quad 3$$

When $x = 1$,

$$A \times 0 + B \times 0 + C \times 1 = -4$$
$$\text{so } C = -4$$

Put $x = 2$ in the identity, $2A + B + 2C = 8 - 6 - 3$

Since $B = 3$ and $C = -4$, $\quad 2A = 4$, $A = 2$

The values $x = 0$ and $x = 1$ were chosen so that all the terms except one in the L.H.S. vanished, leaving equations containing only one unknown. The third value, $x = 2$, was chosen so that the terms, e.g. x^2, were fairly small and easily evaluated.

Exercise 5e

1 Find constants A, B, and C if $4x^2 = Ax(x - 1) + Bx + C$

2 Find constants A, B, and C if $x^2 = Ax(x - 1) + B(x - 1) + Cx$

3 Find constants A and B if $2x = A(x - 1) + B(x - 3)$

4 Is $x(x + 1) - (x + 1)(x - 1) - x = 1$ an equation or an identity?

5 Show that $(x^2 - 1)^2 + (2x)^2 \equiv (x^2 + 1)^2$.

Quadratic equations

If the product of two numbers is zero, then one or other (or both) of those numbers must be zero. So if $(x - 2)(x - 3) = 0$, either $x - 2 = 0$ or $x - 3 = 0$. (Both cannot be equal to zero, as x cannot be equal to 2 and 3 at the same time). If $x - 2 = 0$, then $x = 2$; if $x - 3 = 0$, then $x = 3$, so if

$$(x - 2)(x - 3) = 0, \ x = 2, \text{ or } x = 3$$

To solve quadratic equations, first see if we can factorize them; if so, we can proceed as above.

Example 5.9 *Solve for* x, $x^2 - 7x + 6 = 0$

If
$$x^2 - 7x + 6 = 0$$
$$(x - 1)(x - 6) = 0$$
∴ $\qquad$ either $x - 1 = 0$ or $x - 6 = 0$
∴ $\qquad\qquad\qquad x = 1 \text{ or } 6$

Example 5.10 *Solve for x*, $x^2 - 4x = 0$.

N.B. The factors of this appear to be slightly different from those in Example 5.9. As there is no constant term, x is a common factor.

If
$$x^2 - 4x = 0$$
$$x(x - 4) = 0$$
∴ either $x = 0$ or $x - 4 = 0$
∴ $x = 0$ or $x = 4$

Exercise 5f

Factorize and so solve the following quadratic equations.

1 $x^2 - 5x - 6 = 0$ **2** $x^2 - 7x + 10 = 0$
3 $x^2 + 5x + 6 = 0$ **4** $x^2 + 5x = 0$
5 $3x^2 + 2x = 0$ **6** $3x^2 + 2x - 1 = 0$

Quadratic equations that cannot be factorized easily

If the equations cannot be factorized easily, we have to use a formula. It can be shown that the solutions to

$$ax^2 + bx + c = 0 \qquad (1)$$

are
$$x = \frac{-b \pm \sqrt{(b^2 - 4ac)}}{2a} \qquad (2)$$

so we compare any given equation with (1).

Example 5.11 *Solve, correct to two significant figures*, $3x^2 - 4x - 2 = 0$.

Comparing $3x^2 - 4x - 2 = 0$
with $ax^2 + bx + c = 0$,
$a = 3$, $b = -4$, and $c = -2$. Substituting these values in (2),

$$x = \frac{4 \pm \sqrt{(4^2 - 4 \times 3 \times (-2))}}{6}$$

$$= \frac{4 \pm \sqrt{40}}{6}$$

$$= \frac{4 + 6.324}{6} \text{ or } \frac{4 - 6.324}{6}$$

$$= 1.7 \text{ or } -0.39, \text{ each correct to 2 s.f.}$$

Exercise 5g

Solve the following quadratic equations, correct to two decimal places.

1 $2x^2 + 4x + 1 = 0$

2 $2x^2 - 4x - 1 = 0$

3 $x^2 + x - 4 = 0$

4 $6 - 3x - 2x^2 = 0$

6 Algebra: indices and logarithms, variation, progressions

Indices

$a \times a \times a \times a$ is abbreviated a^4, and $a \times a \times a \ldots$ in which there are n as, is abbreviated a^n. Thus if we are to multiply a^5 by a^4, we are multiplying $a \times a \times a \times a \times a$ by $a \times a \times a \times a$, so we have the product of nine as, written a^9. The number 9 is called the index, and is the sum of the previous indices 5 and 4. Similarly, when dividing products,

$$\frac{a^6}{a^2} = \frac{a \times a \times a \times a \times a \times a}{a \times a} = a^4$$

To *multiply* similar terms, add the indices,

i.e. $\qquad\qquad\qquad a^m \times a^n = a^{m+n}$

To *divide* similar terms, subtract the indices,

i.e. $\qquad\qquad\qquad \frac{a^m}{a^n} = a^{m-n}$

When $m = n$, $\frac{a^m}{a^n} = 1$, so that $a^{m-n} = a^0 = 1$

Use of brackets

To prevent ambiguity, we may have to use brackets. Thus $3x^2$ means $3(x^2)$, and if we wanted to write $3x \times 3x$ we should need to use brackets: $(3x)^2$.

When multiplying expressions containing coefficients as well as indices, take great care to multiply the coefficients and to add (or subtract) the indices.

Example 6.1 *Note the simplification of each of the following.*

$$(a) \quad 2a^3 \times 5a^2 = 10a^5$$

$$(b) \quad \frac{3a^2 \times 4a^3}{2a^4} = \frac{12a^5}{2a^4} = 6a$$

$$(c) \quad \frac{10a^3 \times 2a^4}{4a^7} = \frac{20a^7}{4a^7} = 5$$

But

$$(d) \quad \frac{4a^3 + 5a^3}{3a} = \frac{9a^3}{3a} = 3a^2$$

Exercise 6a

1 Simplify (a) $4a^3 \times 3a^4$ (b) $4a^3 \div 3a^4$

(c) $\dfrac{4a^3 + 3a^3}{a^2}$ (d) $\dfrac{2a^4 \times 3a^2}{6a^6}$

2 Find the value of each of the following, given that $a = 6$, $b = -1$, and $n = 2$.

(a) $3ab^n$ (b) $3(ab)^n$ (c) $(3ab)^n$ (d) $(a + 3b)^n$

Fractional indices

Adding the indices, $a^{\frac{1}{2}} \times a^{\frac{1}{2}} = a^1 = a$, so that $a^{\frac{1}{2}}$ is the number that when multiplied by itself is equal to a, the number we call the square root of a.† Similarly, $a^{\frac{1}{3}}$ is the cube root of a, $a^{\frac{1}{4}}$ is the fourth root.

Since $a^{\frac{1}{4}} \times a^{\frac{1}{4}} \times a^{\frac{1}{4}} = a^{\frac{3}{4}}$, $a^{\frac{3}{4}}$ is the cube of the fourth root of a; similarly, $a^{\frac{2}{3}}$ is the square of the cube root of a.

Negative indices

Since $a^n \times a^{-n} = a^0 = 1$, $a^{-n} = \dfrac{1}{a^n}$, for all numbers n.

This is true even when n is a fraction, so that, e.g. $a^{-\frac{1}{2}} = \dfrac{1}{\sqrt{a}}$

Example 6.2 *Given that $a = 4$, $b = 27$, and $c = 64$, note the value of each of the following:*

$$(a) \qquad a^{\frac{1}{2}} = 4^{\frac{1}{2}} = \sqrt{4} = 2$$

$$(b) \qquad b^{\frac{2}{3}} = (\sqrt[3]{27})^2 = 3^2 = 9$$

$$(c) \qquad c^{-\frac{1}{2}} = \frac{1}{c^{\frac{1}{2}}} = \frac{1}{\sqrt{64}} = \frac{1}{8}$$

† By convention, we mean only the positive square root, unless we write ±.

(d) $\qquad a^{\frac{3}{2}} b^{-\frac{3}{2}} c^{\frac{2}{3}} = (4)^{\frac{3}{2}} (27)^{-\frac{1}{3}} (64)^{\frac{1}{3}}$

$$= (\sqrt{4})^3 \times \frac{1}{\sqrt[3]{27}} \times \sqrt[3]{64}$$

$$= 8 \times \tfrac{1}{3} \times 4 = \tfrac{32}{3}$$

Exercise 6b

1 Without the use of tables or calculator, find the exact value of:

(a) $81^{\frac{1}{2}}$ (b) $81^{-\frac{1}{4}}$ (c) $125^{\frac{2}{3}}$ (d) $36^{-\frac{1}{2}}$

(e) 81^0 (f) $16^{\frac{1}{2}}$ (g) $4^{-\frac{3}{2}}$ (h) 9^{-2}

2 Simplify each of the following:

(a) $a^{\frac{1}{2}} \times a^{\frac{3}{2}}$ (b) $a^{\frac{1}{2}} b^{\frac{3}{2}} \times a^{-\frac{1}{2}} b^{\frac{5}{4}}$ (c) $a^{\frac{1}{2}} b^{\frac{3}{4}} \div a^{\frac{1}{2}} b^{-\frac{1}{4}}$

(d) $a^{\frac{1}{2}} b^{\frac{3}{2}} \times a^{-\frac{1}{2}} b^{\frac{1}{2}}$ (e) $a^{\frac{3}{2}} b^{-\frac{3}{2}} \div a^{\frac{1}{2}} b^{-\frac{1}{2}}$

Logarithms

Since $10^2 = 100$, we can introduce the idea of a logarithm by saying that 'the logarithm of 100 to the base 10 is 2' means $10^2 = 100$; 'the logarithm of 8 to the base 2 is 3' follows from $2^3 = 8$. The logarithm of 1000 to the base 10 is 3, of 10 000 to base 10 is 4. The logarithm of a number to any given base is merely the power to which the base must be raised to give the number,
i.e.

$$\log_{10} x = y \Longleftrightarrow 10^y = x$$
and $\qquad\qquad \log_a x = y \Longleftrightarrow a^y = x.$

We can easily calculate $\log_{10} 100$, $\log_{10} 1000$, $\log_{10} 10\,000$ and so we can obtain tables of logarithms, base 10, or they are available on most calculators. Before calculators were readily available, logarithms were helpful for calculations requiring multiplication and division, but now logarithms are little used for that purpose. The logarithmic function, though, is of considerable importance in later mathematics.

Indices and logarithms

If $\qquad a^m = x$ and $a^n = y$, $\log_a x = m$ and $\log_a y = n$.

Since $\qquad\qquad a^m \times a^n = a^{m+n}$, $xy = a^{m+n}$

$$\log_a xy = m + n,$$

i.e. $\qquad\qquad\qquad \log_a xy = \log_a x + \log_a y$ (1)

Similarly, since $\quad a^m \div a^n = a^{m-n}$

$$\log_a (x/y) = \log_a x - \log_a y$$ (2)

From (1), when $y = x$, $\log_a x^2 = \log_a x + \log_a x = 2 \log_a x$, and extending this, $\log_a(x^n) = n \log_a x$ (3)

These three rules illustrate some of the most interesting properties of the logarithmic function.

Example 6.3 (a) $\log_{10} 2 + \log_{10} 50 = \log_{10} 100 = 2$,
                (b) $\log_2 32 - \log_2 8 = 5 - 3 = 2$,
                (c) $\log_2 (1.6) + \log_2 (20) = \log_2 (32) = 5$.

Example 6.4 *Given that $log_{10} 2 = 0.3010$ and $log_{10} 3 = 0.4771$ correct to 4 d.p., calculate without tables or calculator (a) log_{10} 12, (b) log_{10} (1.5), each correct to 3 d.p.*

(a) Since $12 = 2^2 \times 3$,

$$\log 12 = 2 \log 2 + \log 3$$
$$\log_{10} 12 = 2 \times 0.3010 + 0.4771$$
$$= 1.0791$$
$$= 1.079, \text{ to 3 d.p.}$$

(b) Since $1.5 = 3 \div 2$,

$$\log 1.5 = \log 3 - \log 2$$
$$\log_{10} 1.5 = 0.4771 - 0.3010$$
$$= 0.1761$$
$$= 0.176, \text{ to 3 d.p.}$$

Exercise 6c

1 Simplify each of the following:

(a) $\log_{10} 4 + \log_{10} 25$ (b) $\log_{10} 1250 - \log_{10} 5 + \log_{10} 4$
(c) $\log_4 32 - \log_4 (\frac{1}{2})$ (d) $\log_{10} 25 + \log_{10} 16 - \log_{10} (0.4)$

2 Given that $\log_2 3 = 1.5850$ and $\log_2 5 = 2.3219$, each correct to 4 d.p., find, correct to 3 d.p.,

(a) $\log_2 6$ (b) $\log_2 10$ (c) $\log_2 (0.6)$
(d) $\log_2 1.2$ (e) $\log_2 25$ (f) $\log_2 75$

Variation

If a man walks at a constant speed, the distance travelled is directly proportional to the time taken. Within certain limits, the extension in a piece of elastic is directly proportional to the force applied.

These statements can be written

distance $(s) \propto$ time (t), i.e. $s = kt$

and   extension $(x) \propto$ force (F), i.e. $x = c\,F$,

k and c being constants. These illustrate one of the simplest forms of variation, when two quantities are directly proportional, one to the other.

Since the area A of a circle is πr^2, where r is the radius, the area is proportional to the square of the radius; the volume of a sphere is $\frac{4}{3}\pi r^3$, so the volume is proportional to the cube of the radius.

Inverse proportion

If we travel a fixed distance at a constant speed, the faster we travel, the shorter the time taken on the journey. In this case, the time (t) is inversely proportional to the speed v, $t \propto \dfrac{1}{v}$, i.e. $t = \dfrac{k}{v}$

Example 6.5 *Write down algebraic equations to describe the following examples of variation:*

(a) the momentum M of a body is directly proportional to the velocity v.

$$M \propto v, \text{ i.e. } M = kv$$

(b) Under certain circumstances, the current i in an electrical circuit is inversely proportional to the resistance R.

$$i \propto \frac{1}{R} \text{ i.e. } i = k/R$$

(c) The time t taken for a bus journey of a fixed distance is proportional to the square root of the number n of passengers.

$$t \propto \sqrt{n}, \text{ i.e. } t = k\sqrt{n}$$

Example 6.6 *The time taken by a certain cook to roast a joint of meat is partly proportional to the mass of the joint and partly constant. A joint mass 3 kg is cooked for $2\frac{1}{4}$ hours; a joint mass 4 kg is cooked for 2 hours 55 minutes. Find a formula relating the time t hours and the mass M kg of the joint.*

Since the time t hours is partly proportional to the mass M, and partly constant,

$$t = kM + c, \; k \text{ and } c \text{ being constants.}$$

When $M = 3, t = 2\frac{1}{4}$

$$2\tfrac{1}{4} = 3k + c \tag{1}$$

When $M = 4, t = 2$,

$$2\tfrac{11}{12} = 4k + c$$

Subtracting, $k = \tfrac{2}{3}$. Substituting in (1), $c = \tfrac{1}{4}$, so the formula is

$$t = \tfrac{2}{3}M + \tfrac{1}{4}$$

Exercise 6d

1 Write each of the following statements as an equation.

(a) The interest I paid on a fixed sum of money is proportional to the time t years for which it is invested.

(b) The kinetic energy (T joules) of a body is directly proportional to the square of the velocity (v m s^{-1}).

(c) The time t days taken to construct a length of road is inversely proportional to the square root of the number n of men employed.

2 The safe speed for a car to round a corner is proportional to the square root of the radius of the curve. If the safe speed for a curve radius 50 m is 25 km/h, what is the safe speed for a curve of radius 72 m?

Arithmetic progression

If consecutive terms in a given series differ by a constant, the series is called an arithmetic progression, e.g.

$$1, 3, 5, 7 \dots$$
$$1.1, 1.2, 1.3 \dots$$
$$-1, 1\tfrac{1}{4}, 3\tfrac{1}{2}, 5\tfrac{3}{4}, 8 \dots$$

are examples of arithmetic progressions; $1, 1.1, 1.11, 1.111 \dots$ is not an arithmetic progression.

Since the terms in an arithmetic progression have a common difference d, if the first term is a, the progression is

$$a, a + d, a + 2d, a + 3d \dots$$

and the nth term is $a + (n - 1)d$. To find the sum S of the first n terms of the progression, write

$$S = a \qquad\qquad + (a + d) \qquad + (a + 2d) \dots + a + (n - 1)d$$

Reversing the sequence
$$S = a + (n - 1)d + \bar{\ }a + (n - 2)d + a + (n - 3)d \dots + a$$

Adding term by term

$$2S = \{2a + (n-1)d\} + \{2a + (n-1)d\}$$
$$+ \{2a + (n-1)d\} \ldots + \{2a + (n-1)d\}$$
to n terms,

Thus
$$2S = n\{2a + (n-1)d\}$$
$$S = \frac{n}{2}\{2a + (n-1)d\}$$

Writing $\quad a + (n-1)d = l$, the last term, we have

$$S = \frac{n}{2}(a + l)$$

Example 6.7 *The first term of an arithmetic progression is 7 and the thirteenth term is l. Calculate the common difference, and the number n of terms if the sum of the first n terms is zero.*

Denoting the common difference by d, the thirteenth term is $7 + 12d$ (note the 12; $13 - 1$, from $n - 1$).

$$\therefore \qquad\qquad 7 + 12d = 1, \; d = -\tfrac{1}{2}$$

The sum of the first n terms is $\dfrac{n}{2}\{2a + (n-1)d\}$

$$\frac{n}{2}\{14 + (n-1)(-\tfrac{1}{2})\} = 0$$

Since $n \neq 0$ $\qquad 14 + (n-1)(-\tfrac{1}{2}) = 0$
$$28 = n - 1,$$
$$n = 29,$$

The sum of the first 29 terms is zero.

Geometric progression

If consecutive terms in a certain series are in a fixed ratio, then the series is called a geometric progression. Thus

$$1, 2, 4, 8, 16 \ldots$$
$$2, 3, \tfrac{9}{2}, \tfrac{27}{4} \ldots$$
$$4, 2, 1, \tfrac{1}{2} \ldots$$

are geometric progressions; $1, 2, 4, 7 \ldots$ is not a geometric progression. If the first term is a and the common ratio is r, then the geometric progression can be written

$$a, ar, ar^2, ar^3 \ldots$$

and the nth term will be $a\,r^{n-1}$.

To find the sum S of the first n terms, write

$$S = a + ar + ar^2 + ar^3 + ar^4 \ldots + ar^{n-1}$$

Multiplying by r,

$$rS = ar + ar^2 + ar^3 + ar^4 \ldots + ar^{n-1} + ar^n$$

Subtracting

$$(1 - r)S = a - ar^n$$

$$S = a\frac{1 - r^n}{(1 - r)}$$

Example 6.8 *The second term of a geometric progression is 4 and the fifth term is $13\frac{1}{2}$. Find (a) the common ratio, (b) the first term, (c) the sixth term.*

(a) With the notation above, the second term is ar, so $ar = 4$, and the fifth term is $13\frac{1}{2}$, so that $ar^4 = 13\frac{1}{2}$, i.e. $\frac{27}{2}$. Dividing, $r^3 = \frac{27}{8}$, i.e. $r = \frac{3}{2}$

(b) Since $ar = 4$ and we have found $r = \frac{3}{2}$, $a = \frac{4}{3}$, the first term is 6.

(c) The sixth term is ar^5, which is r times the fifth term, i.e. $(\frac{3}{2})(\frac{27}{2})$, so the sixth term is $\frac{81}{4}$ or $20\frac{1}{4}$.

If we had been given the second and fourth term, then we should have obtained a value for r^2, and we should have had to note that r could have two values, one positive and one negative. Sometimes to prevent this ambiguity we are told that the geometric progression is a series of positive terms.

Exercise 6e

1 Which of the following is an arithmetic progression?

    (a) $1, 2\frac{1}{2}, 3\frac{1}{3} \ldots$

    (b) $2, 3.5, 5 \ldots$

    (c) $1, 11, 21 \ldots$

    (d) $7, -3, -13 \ldots$

2 Which of the following is a geometric progression?

    (a) $1, -2, 4 \ldots$

    (b) $1, 0, -1 \ldots$

    (c) $-2, 1, -\frac{1}{2} \ldots$

    (d) $4, -2, 0 \ldots$

3 Find the fourth term in the arithmetic progression whose first term is 4 and whose common difference is -1.

4 Find the fifteenth term in the arithmetic progression whose fourteenth term is 101 and whose common difference is -11.

5 Find the fourth term in the geometric progression whose first term is 8 and whose common ratio is $(-\frac{3}{2})$.

6 Find the sixteenth term in the geometric progression whose fourteenth term is 44 and whose common ratio is $\frac{1}{2}$.

7 The first term of a certain arithmetic progression is 2 and the third term is 12. How many terms of the progression must be taken if the sum of the terms is 245?

8 The sum of the first n terms of a certain geometric progression is $2\{1 - (\frac{1}{2})^n\}$. Find (a) the first term, (b) the common ratio, (c) the second term.

7 Graphs

Notes

Straight line graphs

Equations of the form $y = mx + c$ or $ax + by = c$ are represented by straight line graphs; it is sufficient to plot three points to draw these graphs.

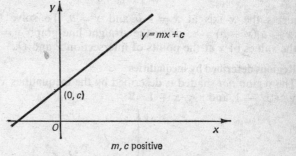

m, c positive

Fig. 7.1

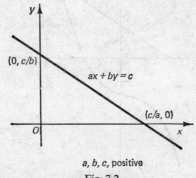

$a, b, c,$ positive

Fig. 7.2

Quadratic graphs

The graph of $y = (x - a)(x + b)$, a and b positive,

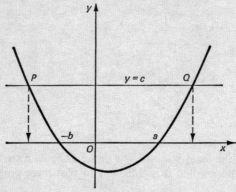

Fig. 7.3

meets the x-axis at $x = -b$ and $x = a$. To solve the equation $(x - a)(x + b) = c$, draw the straight line graph $y = c$, and read the values of x at the points of intersection P and Q.

Regions described by inequalities

The region *not* shaded is described by the inequalities $x > 0$, $y > 0$, $y > x^3 - 1$, and $y < x + 1$.

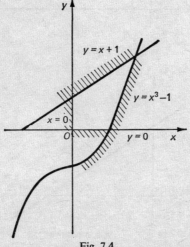

Fig. 7.4

Straight line graphs

A function associates any one element in the domain with one and only one element in the range. Thus the function $f:x \mapsto 3x + 1$ maps 1 into 4, 2 into 7, and 3 into 10 (Fig. 7.5). Since it consists only

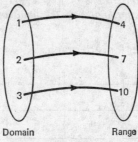

Fig. 7.5

of multiples of x and constants, it is called a *linear* function of x, and may be written $f(x) = 3x + 1$, or $y = 3x + 1$. When we plot the values of y against corresponding values of x, a straight line can be drawn through those points.

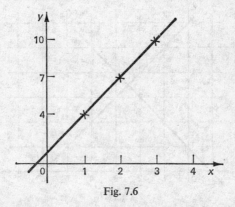

Fig. 7.6

To draw the graph of a linear function, it is quite sufficient to plot three points (as in Fig. 7.6) and draw the straight line through those points. The points can be found taking any easy values of x, not too close, or can be the points at which the straight line crosses the axes, with a third point to check. Thus to draw the graph of $2x + 3y = 6$, when $x = 0$, $y = 2$ and when $y = 0$, $x = 3$; when $x = 1$, $y = 1\frac{1}{3}$, so we can plot these three points.

Two straight lines in general meet in a single point, and the co-ordinates of that point will be the solution of the simultaneous equations describing the straight lines.

Example 7.1 *Draw the graphs of $y = x + 1$ and $y = 6 - x$. Read from the graphs the coordinates of the point of intersection of these straight lines.*

Make a table for values for each graph.

x	0	2	4
$x + 1$	1	3	5
$6 - x$	6	4	2

Generally we are given the range of values to consider, and the scales to use. Here we chose easy positive values of x, to reduce the chance of arithmetic error. We might have had to take, say $x = -2$, if the values obtained for y had not fitted on the axes.

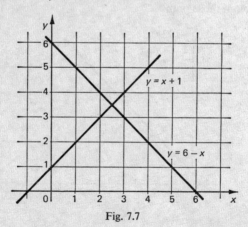

Fig. 7.7

Plot the points and draw the straight lines through them. They can be seen to intersect at $(2\frac{1}{2}, 3\frac{1}{2})$. Thus the solution of the simultaneous equations $y = x + 1$ and $y = 6 - x$ is $x = 2\frac{1}{2}, y = 3\frac{1}{2}$.

Exercise 7a

Draw the graphs of the following straight lines, for values of x from
-4 to 4. Take 2 cm to 1 unit on each axis. Write down the coordinates
of the point of intersection of each pair of straight lines.

1 $y = \frac{1}{2}x + 1, y = 2 - x$ **2** $y = x + 2, y = 3 - x$
3 $y = 2x - 1, y = 2 - 2x$ **4** $y = \frac{1}{2}x - 1, y = -x.$

Other graphs

Graphs required at this level are usually of a few standard types, and
it helps to know the shape to expect, in case of error in calculating the
values of y.

Quadratic function,
e.g. $\qquad\qquad\qquad y = ax^2 + bx + c$

                a positive   *a* negative

Fig. 7.8

Cubic function,
e.g. $\qquad\qquad\qquad y = ax^3 + bx^2 + cx + d$

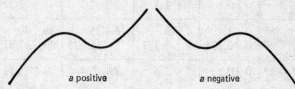

               a positive   *a* negative

Fig. 7.9

(Some cubics do not have such large bends in the middle)

Hyberbola,
e.g. $\qquad\qquad\qquad y = 2 + \dfrac{3}{x}$

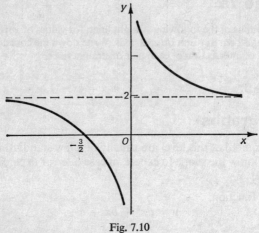

Fig. 7.10

Example 7.2 *Draw the graph of* $y = 4x^2 - x^3$, *plotting points for values of* $x = 0, \frac{1}{2}, 1, 1\frac{1}{2} \ldots 4$. *Take 2 cm to represent 1 unit on the x-axis, and 2 cm to 2 units on the y-axis. Use your graph to find the values of x between 0 and 6 that satisfy* $4x^2 - x^3 = 5$.

Make a table of values, taking particular care when calculating the values when $x = 1.5$, 2.5, etc. (These values are often given in examination papers.) Correct all values of y to 1 decimal place.

x	0	0.5	1	1.5	2	2.5	3	3.5	4
$4x^2$	0	1	4	9	16	25	36	49	64
x^3	0	0.125	1	3.375	8	15.625	27	42.875	64
$y = 4x^2 - x^3$	0	0.9	3	5.6	8	9.4	9	6.1	0

Plot the points, and draw the graph through them. It often helps to draw the graph if you turn the paper to use the natural bend of the wrist.

To find the values of x between 0 and 4 which satisfy $4x^2 - x^3 = 5$, read on the y-axis where $y = 5$, then read the corresponding values of x, marked in Fig. 7.11. Take care to interpret the scales correctly. The values of x are seen to be 1.4 and 3.6.

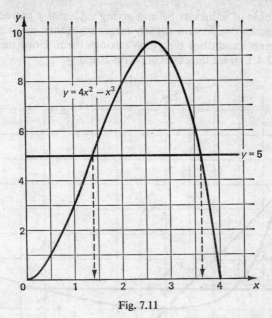

Fig. 7.11

Example 7.3 Draw the graph of $y = \dfrac{x}{3} + \dfrac{3}{x}$, taking a scale of 2 cm for 1 unit on each axis, and plotting points for which $x = 0.5, 1, 2, 3, 4, 5, 6$ and 7.

(i) From your graph, find the range of values of x for which $\dfrac{x}{3} + \dfrac{3}{x}$ is less than 2.4.

(ii) Draw also the graph of $y = 5 - x$. Read the values of x at the point of intersection of these two graphs, and write down the equation in x that is satisfied by these two values of x.

x	0.5	1	2	3	4	5	6	7
$\dfrac{x}{3}$	0.17	0.33	0.67	1	1.33	1.67	2	2.33
$\dfrac{3}{x}$	6	3	1.5	1	0.75	0.6	0.5	0.43
$y = \dfrac{x}{3} + \dfrac{3}{x}$	6.17	3.33	2.17	2	2.08	2.27	2.5	2.76

Make a table of values as before, giving values of y correct to two decimal places (we have a slightly larger scale than in Example 2). Plot the points and draw the graph through them. Draw the straight line $y = 2.4$, to meet the curve in points P and Q.

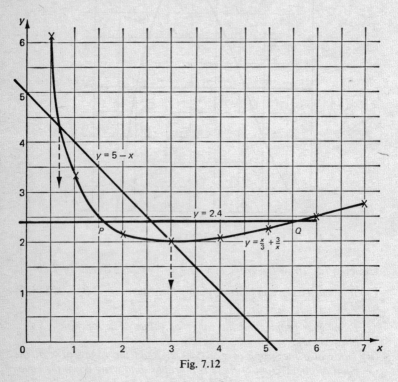

Fig. 7.12

For all points on the curve between P and Q, the value of $\frac{x}{3} + \frac{3}{x}$ is less than 2.4, so the range of values is $1.6 < x < 5.6$.

Now draw the straight line $y = 5 - x$. Taking easy values of x, when $x = 1$, $y = 4$; when $x = 3$, $y = 2$, when $x = 5$, $y = 0$. This meets the curve at points S and T, whose x coordinates are 0.75 and 3 respectively. Where $y = 5 - x$ and $y = \frac{x}{3} + \frac{3}{x}$ meet, then $5 - x = \frac{x}{3} + \frac{3}{x}$, and this is the equation whose roots are 0.75 and 3. The equation can often be left in this form, or simplified by multiplying both sides by $3x$ to give $4x^2 - 15x + 9 = 0$.

N.B. Always mark clearly the points on the graph at which the readings are taken, and take care when reading and interpreting the scale used.

Exercise 7b

On paper 28 cm × 20 cm, use the scale given in each question. The scale on the x-axis is given first.

1 (2 cm to 1 unit on each axis.) Draw the graph of $y = \frac{1}{2}(x + 2)(x - 3)$ for the following values of x: $-3, -2, -1, 0, \frac{1}{2}, 1, 2, 3$, and 4. Use your graph to solve the equations
   (a) $\frac{1}{2}(x + 2)(x - 3) = 1$,
   (b) $(x + 2)(x - 3) = 3$.

2 (5 cm to 1 unit; 1 cm to 1 unit). Copy and complete the table below, to draw the graph of $y = 3x + \dfrac{1}{x}$ for values of x from 0.1 to 2. Use your graph

   (a) to find the range of values of x for which $3x + \dfrac{1}{x} \leqslant 5$,

   (b) to solve the equation $3x + \dfrac{1}{x} = 5 - x$.

x	0.1	0.2	0.5	1	1.25	1.5	2
$3x$	0.3	0.6			3.75	4.5	
$\dfrac{1}{x}$	10.0	5.0			0.8	0.67	
$y = 3x + \dfrac{1}{x}$	10.3	5.6			4.55	5.17	

3 (2 cm to 1 unit; 2 cm to 4 units.) Draw the graph of $y = x^3 - 4x$ for values of x from -3 to $+3$ inclusive. Draw also the graph of $y = x + 1$.

   (a) Find the range of values of x for which $x^3 - 4x \leqslant x + 1$
   (b) Show that the values of x at which the graphs intersect are the solutions of $x^2 - 5 - \dfrac{1}{x} = 0$, and draw another straight line graph to enable you to read the solutions to $x^2 - 5 - \dfrac{2}{x} = 0$.
   (c) Shade the region on the graph satisfying the inequalities $y \geqslant x^3 - 4x$, $y \leqslant x + 1$, and $x \geqslant 0$.

8 Inequalities: graphical representation, linear programming

Notes

$<$ is less than
  e.g. $x < 2$ reads 'x is less than 2'
$\leqslant$ is less than or equal to
  e.g. $x \leqslant 3$ reads 'x is less than or equal to 3'
$>$ is greater than
  e.g. $x > 4$ reads 'x is greater than 4'
$\nless$ is not less than
  e.g. $x \nless 5$ reads 'x is not less than 5'

Shading of regions

Shade the outer boundary of the region *not* required, e.g. unshaded region is described by $y < x$;

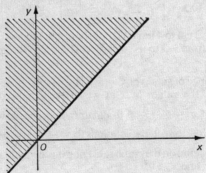

Fig. 8.1

Unshaded region described by $0 < y$

$$0 < x < 4$$
$$x + 2y < 8;$$

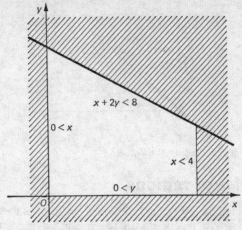

Fig. 8.2

Graphical inequalities

The straight line $y = 1$ passes through all points whose y coordinate is 1. The unshaded half-plane in Fig. 8.3. contains all points

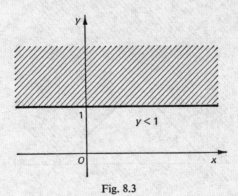

Fig. 8.3

whose y coordinate is less than 1, and so is described by $y < 1$. Similarly, the unshaded half-plane in Fig. 8.4 contains all the points whose y coordinate is less than their x coordinate, and so is described by $y < x$.

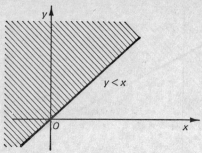

Fig. 8.4

Boundaries of regions

The unshaded region in Fig. 8.5 is bounded by the lines $y = 0$, $y = x$, and $x + y = 4$. All the points in the region have positive y co-ordinates and so are described by $y > 0$. All are such that their y coordinate is less than their x coordinate. (Take any one point, say (2, 1) and verify this.) All are such that $x + y < 4$. Again, notice

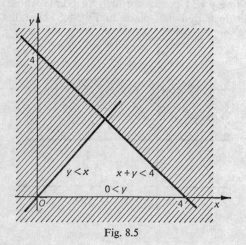

Fig. 8.5

with the point $(2, 1):2 + 1 < 4$. If we select a point outside the region, say (3, 2), we find that it does not satisfy all these conditions, e.g. $3 + 2 \not< 4$.

Shading of regions

Since we are usually interested in the points inside a given region and we do not wish to obscure those points, we generally shade the outside boundary of the region.

Example 8.1 *Shade the outside boundary of the region described by* $x \geqslant 0, y \geqslant 0$ *and* $3x + 2y \leqslant 6.$

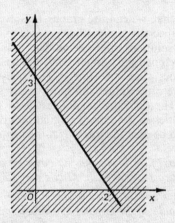

Fig. 8.6

To draw the straight line $3x + 2y = 6$, find the points at which it meets the coordinate axes. When $x = 0, y = 3$; when $y = 0, x = 2$. A third point checks when $x = 1, y = 1.5$.

When trying to find which half-plane we want, the origin $(0, 0)$ is often the easiest point to use; since $3 \times 0 + 2 \times 0 < 6$, we require the half-plane containing the origin, so we shade the side of $3x + 2y = 6$ *not* containing the origin.

Exercise 8a

Take a scale of 2 cm to 1 unit, and draw small sketch-graphs to illustrate each of the following:

1 Shade the outer boundary of the half-planes described by

   (a) $y < x$ (b) $y < x + 1$ (c) $y < x + 3$

2 Shade the outer boundary of the half-planes described by

   (a) $2x + y < 0$ (b) $2x + y < 2$ (c) $2x + y < 4$

3 Shade the outer boundary of the region described by the four inequalities

   $0 < x < 4,\quad y > 0,\quad 2x + 3y < 12$

4 Shade the outer boundary of the region described by the four inequalities

   $x > 1,\quad y > 1,\quad x + 2y < 9,\quad 2x + y < 9.$

Linear programming

In the same way that we can use graphs to solve equations, so we can use graphs, especially straight line graphs, to describe regions in which to look for solutions of problems. This branch of mathematics has only been developed since about 1940, and has found its way into school mathematics since the 1960s. The questions set in early examinations were often rather too hard, many should perhaps be avoided at first. The difficulty candidates faced was in finding the algebraic inequalities to describe the situation given in words. It is most important to be able to write down the inequalities accurately.

Example 8.2 *A taxi firm is planning to buy cars of two types, Minis and Maxis. Minis cost £3000 each, Maxis cost £5000.*

(*a*) *If the firm buys x Minis and y Maxis, write down an inequality satisfied by x and y, if the firm has £50 000 to spend on cars.*

(*b*) *If the firm has only 15 drivers, not all of whom can work at the same time, write down another inequality satisfied by x and y.*

(*c*) *The firm knows from past experience that they need at least 5 Minis; write down an inequality satisfied by x.*

(a) To buy x Minis at £3000 each costs £$3000x$,
to buy y Maxis at £5000 each costs £$5000y$;
since they cannot spend more than £50 000

$$3000x + 5000y \leqslant 50\,000,$$

which we can simplify to $3x + 5y \leqslant 50$.

(b) The total number of cars must be less than 15, so $x + y < 15$.

(c) Since they want at least 5 Minis, $x \geqslant 5$.

Points to note

In (a), the firm could spend all the money available, so we include $3x + 5y = 50$, whereas in (b) not all the drivers are available at any one time, so the inequality had only $<$, not $\leqslant$.

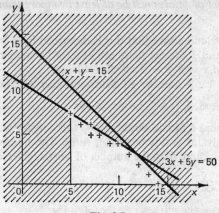

Fig. 8.7

The solutions to this problem correspond to points with integer (i.e. whole number) coordinates. Some of these points are marked $+$, in the unshaded region in Fig. 8.7. It is important to note what restrictions are placed on these points. Problems referring to packs of food often are such that only multiples of 5 or 6 or 10 or 12 are possible; problems referring to numbers of seats in rows usually have similar restrictions. When we have found all the possible solutions, we can then find the best.

Ratios

The hardest inequalities to find are those based on ratio. In Example 8.2, if the firm decided that the number of Minis must be at least twice the number of Maxis, then $x \geqslant 2y$: if it decided that the ratio of Minis to Maxis must be at least 3:2, then $x:y \geqslant 3:2$, i.e. $\dfrac{x}{y} \geqslant \dfrac{3}{2}$, $2x \geqslant 3y$. Always check by seeing whether some arithmetic values satisfy the inequality obtained.

Example 8.3 *With the data of Example 8.2, find the inequalities to describe the following constraints:*

(a) *The number of Minis must be at least twice the number of Maxis.*
(b) *The ratio of the number of Minis to the number of Maxis must be at least 5:4.*

(*c*) *The number of Minis must be at least two more than the number of Maxis.*

(a) We have found above that this is described by $x \geqslant 2y$. If we buy 8 Minis and 3 Maxis, there are at least twice as many Minis as Maxis and $x = 8$, $y = 3$ satisfies $x \geqslant 2y$.

(b) Since the ratio number of Minis:number of Maxis is at least 5:4, $x:y \geqslant 5:4$, $\dfrac{x}{y} \geqslant \dfrac{5}{4}$, i.e. $4x \geqslant 5y$.

11 Minis and 8 Maxis would satisfy this constraint, and $44 > 40$.

(c) This constraint is not based on ratio. The number of Minis is at least two more than the number of Maxis, gives $x \geqslant y + 2$.

Exercise 8b

Write down inequalities to describe the following:

1 A man is planning to grow x tomato plants and y cucumber plants in his greenhouse.

   (a) The total number of plants must not be more than 20.
   (b) Tomatoes cost 25p each and cucumbers 75p each; he must not spend more than £8.
   (c) There must be at least 10 tomato plants.
   (d) There must be at least 4 cucumber plants.
   (e) There must be at least 2 more tomato plants than there are cucumber plants.
   (f) There must be at least twice as many tomato plants as cucumbers.
   (g) He allows 0.8 m² of floor space for each tomato plant and 1 m² for each cucumber; he has only 15 m² of floor space available.

2 A car park is to be laid out for x cars and y lorries.

   (a) There must be room for at least 50 cars.
   (b) The number of lorries must not be more than 20.
   (c) The total number of cars and lorries must not be more than 40.
   (d) Cars are allowed 10 m² of space, lorries 20 m², and there is only 2000 m² available.
   (e) The ratio of the number of cars to the number of lorries must be at least 3:1.
   (f) There must be at least 20 more cars than lorries.

Finding the 'best solution'

Since the inequalities describe a region, not just a point, we usually have several solutions, and can choose the one that is 'best'. If we have to find a profit, we shall usually want to choose the solution that gives as much profit as possible. If we have to find a cost, we shall usually want to have the solution that makes the cost as small as possible.

Example 8.4 *At a school play, the audience is seated partly in chairs and partly on stools. If there are x chairs and y stools, write down inequalities to describe the following constraints:*

(a) *There must be at least 100 seats available.*
(b) *There are only 120 stools available.*
(c) *There must be at least twice as many stools as there are chairs.*
(d) *The school allows 1 m² of floor space for a chair and 0.6 m² for a stool; the area of the floor is 90 m².*

Draw straight line graphs representing these inequalities, and shade the outside boundary of the region in which lie the points corresponding to all possible values of x and y satisfying these conditions. If chairs must be placed in rows in 10 and stools in rows of 12, mark on the diagram all points corresponding to possible numbers of each seat. How many of each type of seat should be provided to make the receipts as large as possible, assuming that all seats provided will be sold, if the prices of tickets are

(e) *70p for a chair and 60p for a stool*
(f) *50p for a chair and 30p for a stool?*

Write down inequalities from the constraints as listed.

(a) Since the total number of seats must be at least 100

$$x + y \geqslant 100.$$

(b) Since there are only 120 stools available

$$y \leqslant 120.$$

(c) There must be at least twice as many stools as chairs

$$y \geqslant 2x$$

 (Check: 20 chairs, 50 stools would satisfy this constraint, and $x = 20, y = 50$ satisfies the inequality).

(d) Since there is only 90 m² of floor space available

$$x + 0.6y \leqslant 90$$

These straight lines are drawn in Fig. 8.8. Since chairs are in rows of 10 and stools in rows of 12, the only possible solutions are those in which x is a multiple of 10 and y a multiple of 12. Points corresponding to these are marked + in Fig. 8.8.

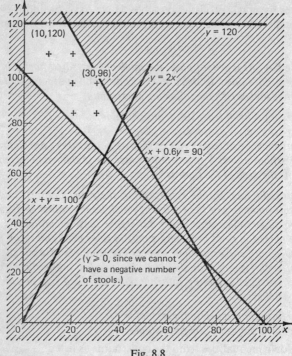

Fig. 8.8

To find the solution that gives most receipts, we shall want to choose large values of x and y. From Fig. 8.8, clearly $x = 30$, $y = 96$ looks likely to be a good possibility, and we calculate that the receipts, at 70p a chair and 60p a stool, would be £78.60. But if we try $x = 10$, $y = 120$ we have receipts of £79.00, a slightly better solution.

On the other hand, if the seats are priced at 50p and 30p, then $x = 30$, $y = 96$ gives £43.80, whereas $x = 10$, $y = 120$ only yields £41, so that for these prices, the best distribution of seats is 30 chairs and 96 stools.

Profit lines

Consider still Example 8.4, and suppose that the prices are 70p for a chair and 50p for a stool. Then if we have x chairs and y stools, the receipts are $(70x + 50y)$ pence. If we provide 40 chairs and 60 stools the receipts would be £58, and the point (40, 60) is seen to lie on the straight line $70x + 50y = 5800$. If we provide 60 of each, the receipts are £72, and the point $(60, 60)$ lies on the line $70x + 50y = 7200$. Clearly these receipt lines are all parallel, and the further the lines are from the origin, the greater the receipts.

Draw any one receipt line $70x + 50y$ equals any constant, (even zero), and then draw the line parallel to this, through a point that is a possible solution.

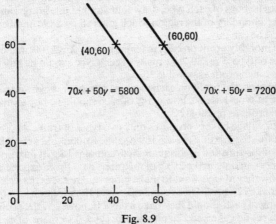

Fig. 8.9

The line furthest from the origin passing through one of the points × gives the best solution. Here we see that $70x + 50y = 6700$ passes through the point $(10, 120)$, and is slightly nearer the origin than $70x + 50y = 6900$, through the point $(30, 96)$, so that, at these prices, 10 chairs and 120 stools is not quite as profitable an arrangement as 30 chairs and 96 stools. Although these lines, giving quantities that we want to make as large as possible, (i.e. maximize) do not necessarily represent profits, these are usually called 'profit lines'. Quantities that we want to minimize, make as small as possible, we usually find by drawing 'cost lines', as close as possible to the origin.

Although profit lines and cost lines are very useful in solving harder problems, many find that at O level stage, trial and error of the likely solutions is usually a simpler method.

Exercise 8c

1 A small businessman is equipping a factory with two types of machine, X and Y. Each machine of type X needs 10 m² of floor space and each machine of type Y needs 7 m²; he has 150 m² available.
Machines X cost £500 each, machines Y cost £1200 each; he has £16 000 to spend on machines.

Write down two inequalities from this data. Using the extra inequalities $x \geqslant 0$ and $y \geqslant 0$, where x and y are the number of machines he buys of each type, draw four straight line graphs and shade the outer boundary of the region which gives all possible numbers of each type he can buy.

If the monthly profit on each machine of type X is £100, and on each machine of type Y is £80, how many of each type should he buy to make as much profit as possible?

If, however, the profit on each machine of type X is £90 and each machine of type Y is £60, how many of each should he buy to make as much profit as possible?

2 A certain village bakery produces only two types of fruit cake, round and square; the mixture in each is the same. Round cakes contain 0.75 kg of mixture and each square cake contains 1 kg of mixture; the bakery can only make 24 kg of mixture a day. From experience, they know they always want to make more square cakes than round. If they make 12p profit on a round cake, and 13p profit on a square cake, how many of each should they bake a day? If, however, the profit is 13p on a round cake and 12p on a square cake, how many of each should they bake a day? (Assume all cakes baked are sold).

3 A schoolmaster is planning to retire and run a holiday kennel for dogs and cats. He estimates that each dog needs 10 m² of space and each cat 7 m²; he has 150 m² available. He intends to have more cats than dogs, but does not wish the ratio of the number of cats to the number of dogs to be greater than 3:2. Write down three inequalities to describe these constraints.

How many of each should he plan to have to accommodate as many animals as possible?

9 Sets and set notation

Mathematical structure

Notation

$\{\ \}$	the set of
$n\{A\}$	the number of elements in the set A
$\{x:\ \}$	the set of elements x such that
$\in$	is an element of
$\notin$	is not an element of
$\mathscr{E}$ (or $\mathscr{U}$)	the universal set
$\varnothing$	the empty (null) set
$\cup$	union
$\cap$	intersection
$\subset$	is a subset of
A'	the complement of the set A
PQ	the operation Q followed by the operation P
$f\colon x \mapsto y$	the function mapping the set X (the domain) into the set Y (the range)
f^{-1}	the inverse of the function f
$\mathbf{R}$	the set of all real numbers
$\mathbf{Z}$	the set of all integers
$\mathbf{Z}_+$	the set of all positive integers
$\mathbf{Q}$	the set of all rationals, e.g. $\frac{3}{4}$

Set theory

A **set** is a well-defined class of objects, so that we can tell without ambiguity whether any one object does or does not belong to that class.

The **empty** (or **null**) set is the set without any elements.

Any element(s) chosen from a set form a **subset** of that set; all subsets except the set itself and the empty set are called **proper** subsets.

Those elements common to two sets A, B, form a set called the **intersection** of A and B, written $A \cap B$; those elements in either A or B or both form a set called the **union** of A and B, written $A \cup B$.

The **complement** of a set A is the set of all elements in the universal set $\mathscr{E}$ which are not in A, and is denoted by A'.

The **cardinal number** of a set A is the number of elements in A, and is written $n\{A\}$; sometimes $n(A)$ is used by other writers.

Binary operations
A **binary operation** * is defined on two elements of a given set S, e.g. 'add 3 to 4', 'divide 5 by 6'.

A set S is **closed** under an operation * if $a*b \in S$ for all a, $b \in S$, e.g. when any one integer is added to any integer, their sum is an integer, so that the set **Z** of all integers is closed under addition.

An operation * is **commutative** over S if $a*b = b*a$ for all a, $b \in S$.

An operation * is **associative** over S if $a* (b*c) = (a*b)*c$ for all $a, b, c \in S$.

The **identity** element e for a given operation * is the element such that $a*e = e*a = a$ for all $a \in S$.

The **inverse** (a^{-1}) of an element a is such that $a*a^{-1} = a^{-1}*a = e$.

Groups
A set S is a **group** under an operation * if

1 S is closed under *;
2 the operation * is associative over S;
3 there is an identity element in S;
4 every element $a \in S$ has an inverse $a^{-1} \in S$.

Relations, mappings, functions
A **relation** associates an element x of one set (the **domain** D) with one or more elements y of another set (the **range** R). The range can be the same set as the domain.

The element y is the **image** of x under that relation.

A **function** (mapping) is a relation under which every element in D has one and only one image in R, i.e. it is a one-one or a many-one relation.

A composite function fg is one in which first g maps an element x into $g(x)$, then f maps $g(x)$ into $fg(x)$. The inverse function is $g^{-1}f^{-1}$.

Definition

A **set** is a well-defined class of objects, by which we mean that we can tell whether any one object does or does not belong to the set. Thus we can define 'the set of all even numbers', since we know how to test whether a number is even or not, but we cannot define 'the set of all large numbers' as we do not know whether a number is 'large' or not. The members of a set are called its elements, and when listed are often written inside brackets, e.g.

the set of all positive numbers less than $10 = \{2, 4, 6, 8\}$

Any elements chosen from a set form a **subset** of that set. Elements common to two sets A and B form a set called the **intersection** of A and B, written $A \cap B$: those elements in either A or B (or both) form a set called the **union** of A and B, written $A \cup B$ (see Fig. 9.1.).

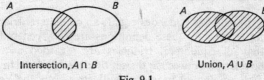

Intersection, $A \cap B$ Union, $A \cup B$

Fig. 9.1

Those elements in the universal set $\mathscr{E}$ that are not in a given set A form a subset A', the **complement** of A.

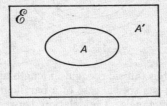

Fig. 9.2

The number of elements in a set is the cardinal number of the set, written $n\{A\}$ or sometimes $n(A)$. Many examination questions test knowledge of either the properties of numbers (*see* p. 9) or elementary geometry, and require as a start the listing of elements in given sets.

Example 9.1   *If the universal set* $\mathscr{E} = \{integers\ n: 4 \leqslant n \leqslant 20\}$
$P = \{primes\}$, $A = \{multiples\ of\ 2\}$, *and* $B = \{multiples\ of\ 3\}$, *list the
elements in each of the sets* (a) P (b) A (c) A' (d) $A' \cap B'$ (e) $(A \cup B)'$.

Since $\mathscr{E}$ is the set of integers between 4 and 20 inclusive,

(a) $P = \{5, 7, 11, 13, 17, 19\}$
(b) $A = \{4, 6, 8, 10, 12, 14, 16, 18, 20\}$
(c) $A' = \{5, 7, 9, 11, 13, 15, 17, 19\}$
(d) Those elements of A' that are also elements of B' are the elements
     in $A' \cap B'$.

So $\qquad\qquad\qquad A' \cap B' = \{5, 7, 11, 13, 17, 19\}$

(e) The elements of B are $\{6, 9, 12, 15, 18\}$ and
     $(A \cup B)'$ is the set of elements not in either A or B (or both),
     i.e. $(A \cup B)' = \{5, 7, 11, 13, 17, 19\}$ the same set as $A' \cap B'$.

Geometrical applications

An isosceles triangle has two sides equal; an equilateral triangle has
all three sides equal, and these definitions are now generally interpreted so that all equilateral triangles are regarded as isosceles
triangles. The relation between I, the set of all isosceles triangles and
T, the set of all equilateral triangles, is illustrated by the Venn diagram below.

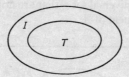

Fig. 9.3

Similarly a rhombus (all sides equal in length as well as opposite
sides being parallel) is a special case of a parallelogram, a square is a
special case of a rectangle. The relation between some sets are
illustrated below, where

$$H = \{all\ rhombuses\}$$
$$P = \{all\ parallelograms\}$$
$$R = \{all\ rectangles\}$$
$$S = \{all\ squares\}$$
and $\qquad C = \{all\ cyclic\ quadrilaterals\}$

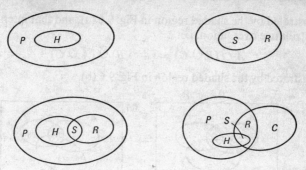

Fig. 9.4

de Morgan's Laws

The result in Example 9.1 (e) illustrates one of de Morgan's Laws, which are

$$(A \cap B)' = A' \cup B',$$
and
$$(A \cup B)' = A' \cap B',$$

and can be illustrated by Venn diagrams. In Fig. 9.5 (a), the shaded region represents either $(A \cap B)'$ or $A' \cup B'$, and in Fig. 9.5 (b), the shaded region represents either $(A \cup B)'$ or $A' \cap B'$.

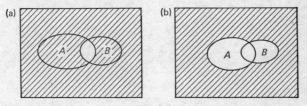

Fig. 9.5

In a similar manner, Venn diagrams can be used to illustrate that the operations of forming the union or the intersection of sets are commutative, associative and distributive, i.e.

commutative,
$$A \cup B = B \cup A \quad \text{and} \quad A \cap B = B \cap A,$$
and associative,
$$A \cup (B \cup C) = (A \cup B) \cup C \text{ and } A \cap (B \cap C) = (A \cap B) \cap C.$$

That union is distributive over intersection, i.e.

$$A \cup (B \cap C) = (A \cup B) \cap (A \cup C)$$

is illustrated by the shaded region in Fig. 9.6 (a), and that intersection is distributive over union, i.e.

$$A \cap (B \cup C) = (A \cap B) \cup (A \cup C)$$

is illustrated by the shaded region in Fig. 9.6 (b).

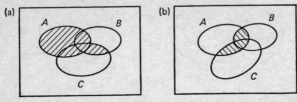

Fig. 9.6

Exercise 9

1 If $\mathcal{E} = \{$all integers $n: 1 \leqslant n \leqslant 12\}$, $A = \{$multiples of 2$\}$, $B = \{$multiples of 4$\}$, and $P = \{$primes$\}$, list the elements in (a) A (b) B (c) $A \cap B$ (d) $P \cap A'$.   *Remember that 1 is not a prime.*
   Find also (e) $n\{P\}$ (f) $n\{P \cap B\}$.
2 If $\mathcal{E} = \{$all triangles$\}$, $I = \{$all isosceles triangles$\}$, and $R = \{$all right-angled triangles$\}$, draw a Venn diagram to illustrate the relation between the sets. Find the angles in all triangles in the set $I \cap R$.

10 Binary operations and groups

Binary operations

'Multiply 6 by 4', 'Add 2 to 3'. These are examples of binary operations being performed on elements of the set of real numbers **R**, by which two elements of **R** are combined according to some clearly-defined rule. The rule may be stated in words, as above, or in symbols, e.g. 6×4, $2 + 3$. A binary operation is often denoted by *.

Example 10.1 *A binary operation * is defined over* **R**, *the set of all real numbers, that* $x * y = x - 2y$. *for all* $x, y \in$ **R**. *Find* $x*y$ *(a) if* $x = 4, y = 2, (b)$ *if* $x = 2, y = 4$.

Since
$$x * y = x - 2y,$$
$$4 * 2 = 4 - 2 \times 2 = 0,$$
and
$$2 * 4 = 2 - 2 \times 4 = -6.$$

Commutative

If the order in which the elements are combined does not affect the result, the operation is **commutative**. Thus addition is commutative, for $a + b = b + a$, multiplication is commutative, for $a \times b = b \times a$, but subtraction is not commutative, for $a - b \neq b - a$, nor is the operation * defined in Example 10.1 commutative, for $2 * 4 \neq 4 * 2$.

Associative

If we wish to combine three elements in a binary operation, we have to combine them in pairs. Thus to add $2 + 3 + 4$ we first decide whether to add 2 and 3 then add 4 to the result, or whether to add 3 and 4 then add 2 to that result. If the order does not affect the result, the operation is called **associative**. Expressed algebraically, the operation * is associative if

$$a * (b * c) = (a * b) * c$$

for all a, b, c in the set S on which the operation is defined.

Closure

If we add two integers the sum is an integer; if we multiply two integers, the result is an integer. But if we divide one integer by another, the result may not be integer, for $6 \div 2 = 3$, but $6 \div 4 = 1\frac{1}{2}$. The set of integers **Z** is said to be closed under addition and multiplication, but not under division. Expressed algebraically, a set S is closed under a binary operation * if $a * b$ belongs to S, for all a, b belonging to S.

Example 10.2 (a) *The set of all even numbers is closed under addition, under subtraction, and under multiplication.*

(b) *The set of all odd integers is not closed under addition and subtraction, but is closed under multiplication.*

(c) *The set of all numbers that are powers of 2, e.g.* 2^1, 2^2, *is not closed under addition or subtraction, but is closed under multiplication.*

Identity element

When zero is added to any number, the value of that number is unaltered. When any number is multiplied by 1, that number is unaltered. Zero is called the identity element under addition; 1 is the identity element under multiplication. The identity element (usually denoted by e) has the property that $a * e = e * a$ for all a.

Inverse element

$2 \times \frac{1}{2} = 1$; 1 is the identity element for multiplication, and $\frac{1}{2}$ can be called the 'multiplicative inverse' of 2. The inverse of an element a under an operation * is that element (usually denoted by a^{-1}) such that $a * a^{-1} = a^{-1} * a = e$. Thus the additive inverse of 2 is -2, since $2 + (-2) = -2 + 2 = 0$, and 0 is the identity element under addition.

Example 10.3 *If $S = \{2, 4, 6, 8, 10, 12\}$, an operation * is defined on S that $a * b$ is the remainder after the product of a and b has been*

divided by 14, *thus* $8 * 12 = 12$, *since* $8 \times 12 = 6 \times 14 + 12$.
(*a*) *Find the identity element.* (*b*) *Find the inverse of* 4 *and the inverse of* 12. (*c*) *Find the inverse of* 10, *and use this result and the fact that the operation is associative to solve the equation* $10 * x = 4$.

(*a*) The identity element must be such that when associated with any number, that number is unaltered. We see from the data of the question that $8 * 12 = 12$. Is 8 the identity? Checking, $8 * 2 = 8$, $8 * 4 = 4$, etc., so that for all elements a, $8 * a = a * 8 = a$, and 8 is the identity element. It is possible to find a proof using algebra, if we wish to avoid checking every element.

(*b*) The inverse a of 4 must be such that $4 * a = 8$, since 8 is the identity element. Clearly $a = 2$. To find the inverse of 12, a little trial and error may be needed to obtain the result that 10 is the inverse of 12.

(*c*) Since 10 is the inverse of 12, 12 will be the inverse of 10.
To solve the equation $10 * x = 4$, use the binary operation * and the element 12, i.e.

$$12 * (10 * x) = 12 * 4$$

Since we are told that * is associative,

$$(12 * 10) * x = 12 * 4$$

But $12 * 10 = 8$, since 12 is the inverse of 10, and 8 is the identity element,

$$8 * x = 12 * 4$$

i.e. $$x = 6$$

We were given that the operation is associative. It is also commutative, and we can show that the set S is closed under this operation.

Exercise 10a

1 The binary operation * is defined on the set $S = \{1, 2, 3, 4\}$ that $a * b$ is the quotient when $(a + b)$ is divided by 2, e.g. $2 * 4 = 3$, and $2 * 3 = 2$.

(a) Find whether the set is closed under *, and whether there is an identity element.
(b) Is the operation commutative or associative?
(c) Find a subset B of S which is closed under *, and another subset C that is not closed under *.
(d) Find two possible values of x such that $3 * x = 3$.

2 The binary operation * is defined on the set of non-negative real numbers S as $a * b = \sqrt{(a^2 + b^2)}$.

   (a) Calculate $3 * (4 * 5)$ and $(3 * 4) * 5$. What does this tell us about the operation *?

   (b) Find the identity element for this operation.

3 The set S consists of four 2 by 2 matrices, of which three are $A = \begin{pmatrix} 1 & 0 \\ 0 & 1 \end{pmatrix}$, $B = \begin{pmatrix} -1 & 0 \\ 0 & -1 \end{pmatrix}$, and $C = \begin{pmatrix} 1 & 2 \\ -1 & -1 \end{pmatrix}$.

   (a) Given that S is closed under matrix multiplication, find the fourth matrix D.

   (b) Find the identity element.

   (c) Find the inverse of B and the inverse of C.

Modular arithmetic

Interesting binary operations can be defined as in Example 10.3, when we write down the remainder after division by a given number. This is called modular arithmetic; the tables below are the addition and multiplication tables mod 14, defined on the set of numbers 2, 4, 6, 8, 10, 12. Carry out the operations and verify that each of the entries is correct.

+	2	4	6	8	10	12
2	4	6	8	10	12	0
4	6	8	10	12	0	2
6	8	10	12	0	2	4
8	10	12	0	2	4	6
10	12	0	2	4	6	8
12	0	2	4	6	8	10

addition mod 14

×	2	4	6	8	10	12
2	4	8	12	2	6	10
4	8	2	10	4	12	6
6	12	10	8	6	4	2
8	2	4	6	8	10	12
10	6	12	4	10	2	8
12	10	6	2	12	8	4

multiplication mod 14

Groups

If a set S of elements is such that

1 S is closed under a binary operation *;
2 the operation is associative over S, i.e.

$$a * (b * c) = (a * b) * c \text{ for all } a, b, c \in S;$$

3 there is an identity element in S;
4 every element a of S has an inverse a^{-1} in S;

then S is said to form a group under *. To show that any one set does not form a group under any given operation *, it is sufficient to show that any one of the above conditions is *not* satisfied. To show that any set is a group under a given operation *, we have to show that all four conditions are satisfied. We can often assume, or we may be told, that the operation is associative, as proving that may be long.

Example 10.4 *Show that the set of odd integers is not a group under addition.*

Since the sum of two odd integers is even, the set of odd integers is not closed under addition, so cannot form a group under addition.

Example 10.5 *Show that the set of odd integers is not a group under multiplication.*

Although the set is now closed under the operation, and there is an identity element, 1, at least one element, say 3, does not have an inverse, so the set cannot be a group.

Example 10.6 *Show that the integers* {2, 4, 6, 8, 10, 12} *form a group under multiplication mod* 14, *given the operation is associative.*

Referring to the multiplication table on p. 92, we see that all the numbers in the table belong to S, so that S is closed.

We have been given that the operation is associative – it would be tedious to prove. We found that 8 was the identity element, and we can see that every element has an inverse. Thus the four conditions for a group are satisfied.

The symmetry of the table shows that the operation is commutative. Commutative groups are called **Abelian groups**.

Exercise 10b

1 Draw up tables to show addition and multiplication mod 4 on the set of numbers $S = \{0, 1, 2, 3\}$. Show that S is a group under one of these operations but not under the other.
2 Draw up tables to show addition and multiplication mod 5 on the set $S = \{0, 1, 2, 3, 4\}$. Show that S does not form a group under multiplication mod 5, but find a subset of S that is a group under multiplication mod 5.

11 Relations and functions

Relations

A relation associates some members of one set (the **domain**) with some members of another set (the **codomain**), and can often be illustrated by a Papy graph, as below. Suppose the domain is the set {2, 3} and the codomain is the set {4, 5, 6}. If the relation is 'less than', then the association between the elements of the domain and the codomain is illustrated by Fig. 11.1. If the relation is 'is a factor of' the relation is illustrated by Fig. 11.2. Notice in the first relation

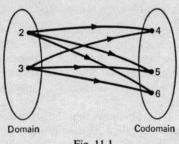

Fig. 11.1

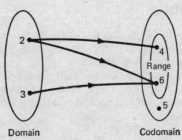

Fig. 11.2

every element of the codomain is associated with some one element of the domain, whereas in the second relation the element 5 is not associated with any element of the domain. Those elements in the codomain which are associated with elements in the domain are said to form the **range** under that relation.

Function

If the relation is 'one less than' then every element in the domain is associated with one and only one element in the range. The association is now called a function. Many of the functions we study can be described algebraically. The function which associates every element in the domain with the element two greater than it is most simply written $f: x \mapsto x + 2$; the function which associates every element with its square is written $f: x \mapsto x^2$. The Papy graphs of functions can

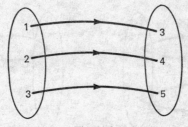

Fig. 11.3

be easily recognized because only one arrow goes from each member of the domain. The function $f: x \mapsto x + 2$ is illustrated in Fig. 11.3, the domain being $\{1, 2, 3\}$.

Mapping

This term should mean exactly the same as function,† but is sometimes incorrectly used to mean 'relation', and so is best avoided.

Inverse function

The function $f: x \mapsto x + 2$ associated every member of a given domain with the corresponding member of the range. The inverse function associates every member of the range with the corresponding member of the domain. Here the inverse function, written f^{-1}, is such that

† *See Mathematical Gazette*, December, 1977.

$f^{-1}:x\mapsto x-2$. Where there may be any confusion, we can refer to elements in the range as y, so that $f^{-1}:y\mapsto y-2$.

Example 11.1 *If $f:x\mapsto x^2$, find* (a) *the range if the domain is* $\{1,4\}$; (b) *the domain if the range is* $\{1, 4\}$.

(a) When $x=1$, $x^2=1$, and when $x=4$, $x^2=16$, so the range is $\{1, 16\}$.
(b) When $x^2=1$, $x=-1$ or 1, and when $x^2=4$, $x=-2$ or $+2$, so that the domain is $\{-2, -1, 1, 2\}$. This is illustrated by the Papy graph below (Fig. 11.4a).

Example 11.2 *If $f:x\mapsto 3x+4$, find the inverse function f^{-1}.*
It may help to denote the image of any element x by y. Then $y=3x+4$, so that $x=\frac{1}{3}(y-4)$. The inverse function is such that $f^{-1}:y\mapsto\frac{1}{3}(y-4)$, or, in terms of x, $f:x\mapsto\frac{1}{3}(x-4)$.

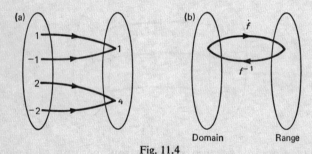

Fig. 11.4

Example 11.3 *If $f:x\mapsto x^2$, find the inverse relation.*

The inverse relation is clearly $f^{-1}:y\mapsto\pm\sqrt{y}$. If the domain contains positive and negative numbers, then each element in the range is

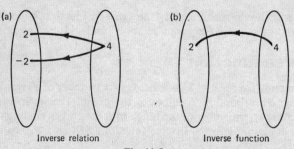

Fig. 11.5

associated with two elements in the domain, and the relation is not a function. If, however, the domain only contains positive numbers (or only negative numbers) then there is no ambiguity, and the inverse relation can be described as a function.

Composite function

The function $f: x \mapsto 3x + 2$ can be described as two separate functions. First an element x is multiplied by 3 then 2 is added. If $g: x \mapsto 3x$ and $h: x \mapsto x + 2$, then $f = hg$. Notice the order. Denote the image of the element 1 under f by $f(1)$. Then from our definition of f, $f(1) = 3 \times 1 + 2$, i.e. $f(1) = 5$. But $g(1) = 3$ and $h(3) = 5$, so that $f(1) = hg(1)$, whereas $h(1) = 3$ and $g(3) = 9$, so that $f(1) \neq gh(1)$. Always read from the element, that is, from right to left. We see similarly that $(gf)^{-1} = f^{-1} g^{-1}$, as in the example following.

Example 11.4 If $f: x \mapsto x + 2$ and $g: x \mapsto \dfrac{1}{x}$, find the inverse functions f^{-1}, g^{-1}. Find $f(2), gf(2) \, fg(2), f^{-1} g^{-1}(2)$ and $g^{-1} f^{-1}(2)$.

Since $f: x \mapsto x + 2, f^{-1}: x \mapsto x - 2$

Since $g: x \mapsto \dfrac{1}{x}, g^{-1}: x \mapsto \dfrac{1}{x}$

Moreover, $f(2) = 4$, so $gf(2) = g(4) = \frac{1}{4}$, whereas $g(2) = \frac{1}{2}$ and $fg(2) = f(\frac{1}{2}) = 2\frac{1}{2}$.

Also $f^{-1} g^{-1}(\frac{1}{4}) = f^{-1}(4) = 2$, but $g^{-1} f^{-1}(\frac{1}{4}) = g^{-1}(-\frac{7}{4}) = -\frac{4}{7}$.

Exercise 11

1 If $f: x \mapsto x + 1$ and $g: x \mapsto \frac{1}{2}x$, find
   (a) $f(1)$, (b) $gf(1)$ (c) $fg(1)$ (d) $f^{-1}(1)$ (e) $g^{-1}(1)$ (f) $f^{-1}g^{-1}(1)$

2 If $f: x \mapsto x - 3$ and $g: x \mapsto \dfrac{2}{x}$, find the inverse functions f^{-1}, g^{-1}. Find also the function $(fg)^{-1}$.

12 Statistics and the representation of data

Notes

'Average'

To find the **mean** of n scores, add them together and divide by n, e.g. the mean of 1, 5, 6 is $\frac{1}{3}(1 + 5 + 6) = 4$.

The **median** is the middle score when arranged in ascending order,

e.g. the median of 1, 6, 5 is 5,
the median of 1, 6, 5, 4 is $\frac{1}{2}(4 + 5) = 4\frac{1}{2}$.

The **mode** is the commonest score, e.g. the mode of 2, 3, 1, 3 is 3.

Pie charts

The angle at the centre of the circle is proportional to the frequency. For example,

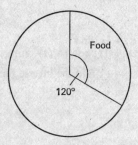

Fig. 12.1

Histograms

The *area* of each rectangle is proportional to the frequency. Check the widths of the rectangles, e.g.

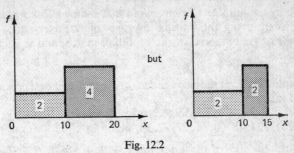

Fig. 12.2

Cumulative frequency curve
This gives the cumulative frequency less than (or less than or equal to) a certain score. Check whether a question requires a reading *less* than or *greater* than a certain score. The median of n scores is

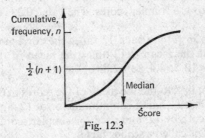

Fig. 12.3

found by reading against a cumulative frequency of $\frac{1}{2}(n + 1)$; if n is large, $\frac{1}{2}n$ may be used.

Average

'The average industrial wage is now £84.90 a week' ... 'His average score last cricket season was 24.9 runs' ... We know that some workers earned less than £84.90 a week, and that some earned more; we know that this batsman certainly did not score 24.9 runs in any innings, let alone every innings. These numbers are merely **statistics** which, interpreted correctly tell us something about the industrial earnings or something about the runs scored by this batsman.

Mean

The commonest way of finding a statistic to give information about a sample is to add all the elements in the sample together, and to divide by the number of elements in that sample. This is the statistic used when giving the batting 'average' of cricketers, the 'average' number of goals scored in each football match, and it is called the **mean**.

Example 12.1 *Find the mean of each of the following sets of scores:*
(a) 1, 1, 2, 4, 5, 5, 6, 6, 7, 7
(b) 1.2, 1.2, 2.2, 4.2, 5.2, 5.2, 6.2, 6.2, 7.2, 7.2
(c) 12, 12, 24, 48, 60, 60, 72, 72, 84, 84

(a) Since the sum of the ten scores 1, 1, 2, 4, 5, 5, 6, 6, 7, 7 is 44, the mean is $\frac{44}{10}$, i.e. 4.4.
(b) The scores in (b) are each 0.2 more than the corresponding scores in (a), so that the mean is 4.4 + 0.2, i.e. 4.6.
   If we had not first found the mean of the scores in (a), we could have subtracted 0.2 from each of the scores in (b) anyway, to enable us to use simpler scores. The value 0.2 is called a **working zero**.
(c) The scores in (c) are each 12 times the corresponding scores in (a), so that the mean is 12 times the mean of the scores in (a), the mean is 12 × 4.4, i.e. 52.8.

If we had not first found the mean of the scores in (a), we could still have noticed that we had a common factor of 12, and so could have divided each score by 12, and used the simpler scores, 1, 1, 2, 4, etc. The number 12 is called a **scaling factor**.

Median

A statistic that is not affected by a few unusual scores of extreme size, either very large or very small, is the **median**. The scores are ranked in order of size, and the middle score is the median. If there are two 'middle' scores, the mean of the two is taken as the median.

Example 12.2 *Find the median of each of the following sets of scores:*
(a) 0, 1, 0, 2, 5, 0, 4; (b) 0, 1, 0, 2, 5, 0, 4, 3.

Rearranging the scores in (a) in ascending order, we have

$$0, 0, 0, \boxed{1}, 2, 4, 5$$
$$\downarrow$$
$$\text{median}$$

The middle one of these is 1, so the median is 1.

When we rearrange the scores in (b), we have

$$0, 0, 0, \boxed{1, 2}, 3, 4, 5$$

$$\text{median is } \frac{1+2}{2}$$

There are eight scores now, so the median is the mean of 1 and 2, i.e. 1.5.

Mode

A third term that is sometimes used to describe a number of scores is the **mode**; this is merely the commonest, the score that occurs most frequently, e.g. the mode of 0, 1, 0, 2, 0, 1, 2, 1, 3, 0 is 0.

Exercise 12a

1 Find the mean, median, and mode of each of the following sets of scores:

(a) 2, 2, 3, 4, 6   (b) 1, 1, 2, 3, 5, 6
(c) 1, 0, 1, 4, 2, 3   (d) 1, 0, 2, 0, 5, 7

2 Find the mean of the following sets of scores:

(a) 1, 1, 3, 5, 7   (b) 0.1, 0.1, 0.3, 0.5, 0.7
(c) 21, 21, 23, 25, 27   (d) 981, 981, 983, 985, 987

3 Find x if the mean of 1, 3, 6, 7 and x is 4.
4 The mean of ten scores is 4. If six of these scores have a mean of 6, find the mean of the other four scores.

Frequency distribution

Consider the scores 1, 1, 1, 1, 2, 2, 2, 3, 4, 4, 4, 4.

To find their mean, we could add all together and divide by 12. We can say that the *frequency* of 1 is four, since there are four scores of 1, that the frequency of 2 is three, since there are three scores of 2, and so on. For large numbers of scores it often helps to make out a frequency table as below:

Scores (x)	Frequency (f)	Product (fx)
11	9	99
12	15	180
13	11	143
14	8	112
15	5	75
16	2	32
	50	641

The total number of scores is the sum of the frequencies, i.e. 50. The sum of all the scores is the total in the third column, i.e. 641, so the mean is 641 ÷ 50, i.e. 12.82.

We may have the frequency of scores in certain **intervals** given, as in this example.

Example 12.3 *A survey taken one day showed the following annual salaries of a sample of travellers at a certain railway station.*

£5000 *or above, and below*	£6000	7
£6000 *or above, and below*	£7000	13
£7000 *or above, and below*	£8000	16
£8000 *or above, and below*	£9000	9
£9000 *or above, and below* £10 000		5

Use mid-interval values to estimate the mean annual salary of these travellers.

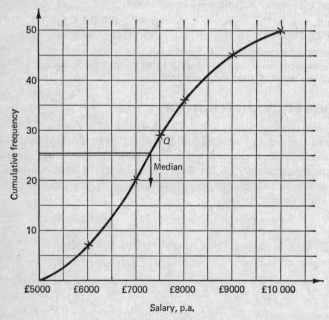

Fig. 12.4

Since we do not know the exact salary of these travellers, we estimate that those travellers with salaries between £5000 and £6000 have a salary of £5500, those in the range £6000–£7000 have a salary of £6500, and so on. Using a working zero of £5500 simplifies the calculations a little, and the calculations should be set out as below:

Score (£x)	£(x − 5500)	f	f(x − 5500)
5500	0	7	0
6500	1000	13	13 000
7500	2000	16	32 000
8500	3000	9	27 000
9500	4000	5	20 000
		50	92 000

$\frac{92\ 000}{50} = 1840$, so the mean is 1840 greater than the working zero,

i.e. 5500 + 1840; the mean salary is £7340.

Notice that if we had been given open intervals, 'below £5000' or 'above £10 000', we should not have known from the data what to take as a mid-interval value, and should have not been able to calculate an estimate of the mean. Sometimes, though, our general knowledge may help to suggest likely boundaries; speeds of cars on roads rarely exceed 110 km h^{-1}.

Cumulative frequency curve

Looking at the data in Example 12.3, we see that

	no traveller had a salary of less than	£5000 p.a.
	7 travellers had a salary of less than	£6000 p.a.
	20 travellers had a salary of less than	£7000 p.a.
	36 travellers had a salary of less than	£8000 p.a.
	45 travellers had a salary of less than	£9000 p.a.
and	50 travellers had a salary of less than	£10 000 p.a.

The figures in the left hand column are the **cumulative** sums of the frequencies in Example 12.3, and the curve displaying these is called a cumulative frequency curve (Fig. 12.4).

We usually join the points we have plotted by a smooth curve; if a series of straight lines is used, that assumes the salaries are evenly spread over each interval, whereas we might expect that of the nine travellers with salaries in the range £8000–£9000, more than half would have a salary nearer to £8000 than to £9000.

Using our cumulative frequency curve, we can estimate that 15 travellers had a salary below £6600, in particular that half the travellers had a salary below £7300. This last estimate suggests that the median will be about £7300. Strictly, as we have 50 scores, the median is between the 25th and the 26th score, but with larger samples than this, e.g. 500 scores, the difference is negligible and we can read the halfway score as the median. Only travellers earning more than £7500 can join the Luncheon Club. How many of our travellers are eligible? Reading across at Q, we have the cumulative frequency of 29. This tells us that 29 travellers earn below £7500, so that 21 will earn above. Thus 21 travellers can belong to the Luncheon Club.

N.B. Always note whether readings *above* or *below* a given value are required. To pass an examination, candidates have to score *more* than a certain mark; if eggs are to be graded as large, their mass has to be *greater* than a given mass; to be graded as small, their mass has to be *less* than a given mass.

Exercise 12b

1 The marks of 500 candidates in a GCE examination are given below:

Marks	0–9	10–19	20–9	30–9	40–9	50–9	60–9	70–9	80–9	90–9
Number of candidates	8	17	28	38	60	78	110	70	54	37

(a) Taking mid-interval values of 4.5, 14.5, etc., calculate an estimate of the mean mark scored by these candidates.

(b) Draw a cumulative frequency curve for this distribution and use it to estimate

  (i) the median mark;

 (ii) the mark exceeded by 30% of these candidates (called the 30th percentile);

(iii) the number of candidates who passed, if the pass mark was 44%.

2 A certain firm recorded the number of letters posted each day over a period of 100 days:

Number of letters	0–19	20–29	30–39	40–49	50–59
Number of days	9	23	38	27	3

(a) Taking mid-interval values of 9.5, 24.5, 34.5, etc., calculate an estimate of the mean number of letters posted in a day.

(b) Draw a cumulative frequency curve for this distribution and estimate

   (i) the median number of letters posted in one day;
   (ii) on how many days more than 45 letters were posted.

Representation of data

Pie chart

When data has been collected, we may wish to use a diagram to display this data in a clear and attractive manner, as in Fig. 12.5

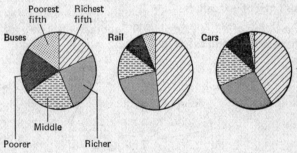

The rich travel: percentage spending on each mode of travel accounted for by each income group.

Fig. 12.5

which displays famous data collected by *The Economist* to show that transport, both public and private, is used more by the richer socio-economic groups than by the poorer, perhaps suggesting that transport subsidies help mainly the rich. These diagrams are called pie-charts or, sometimes, circular diagrams. Since the area of each section is proportional to the angle of the centre of the circle, the ratio of the angles is made equal to the ratio of the quantities displayed in the diagram. This diagram represents most clearly different proportions of a whole, e.g. the number of lessons a week spent on each subject in school, the fractions of an income spent on rent, food, clothing, etc.

Example 12.4 *A consumer agency noted that in one year* 500 *of its callers complained once,* 200 *complained twice,* 50 *complained three times,* 50 *complained four times, and* 100 *complained five or more times. Draw a pie-chart to display this data.*

There were 900 callers at this agency

so that
$$900 \text{ callers will be represented by } 360°$$

$$500 \text{ callers by } \frac{500}{900} \times 360°, \text{ i.e. by } 200°$$

$$200 \text{ callers by } \frac{200}{900} \times 360°, \text{ i.e. by } 80°$$

$$50 \text{ callers by } \frac{50}{900} \times 360°, \text{ i.e. by } 20°$$

$$50 \text{ callers by } \frac{50}{900} \times 360°, \text{ i.e. by } 20°$$

$$100 \text{ callers by } \frac{100}{900} \times 360°, \text{ i.e. by } \underline{40°}$$

$$\overline{360°}$$

Check: Total of 900 callers.

Draw a sector of a circle, angle 200°, another angle 80°, and so on, and mark the diagram as in Fig. 12.6.

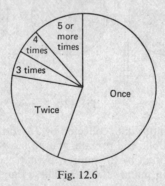

Fig. 12.6

Histogram

Probably the commonest type of diagram is like Fig. 12.7, which shows the assets of a small Building Society. The area of each rectangle is proportional to the amount of money it represents. *If the rectangles are of equal width*, as is often the case, then the length of each rectangle will be proportional to the amount represented. This must not make us think that the length is *always* proportional to the amount represented. Check carefully whether the class-intervals

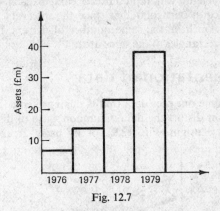

Fig. 12.7

have the same width. It may well be realistic to have different width class intervals, and many GCE questions on histograms test this.

Example 12.5 *A sample of* 100 *drivers were asked how far they were planning to drive on that journey, and their replies recorded below:*

	Less than 5 km	5 km– 10 km	10 km– 20 km	20 km– 30 km	30 km– 40 km
Number of drivers	4	16	16	24	40

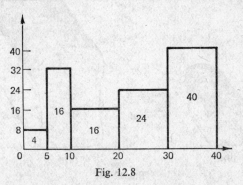

Fig. 12.8

Notice that the first two class-intervals are of width 5 km, the others width 10 km. In Fig. 12.8, if we mark the x-axis as shown and take a scale of 2 cm to represent 10 cars in each of the first two intervals, then 2 cm of length will represent 20 cars in each of the other intervals. Notice in particular that since the intervals 5 km–10 km and 10 km–20 km have the same number of drivers, they must be represented by rectangles of the same area.

Misrepresentation of data

From time to time one sees data that is misrepresented; represented by diagrams that distort the data. Common ways of distorting data are using a false origin (Fig. 12.9), or by using areas or volumes

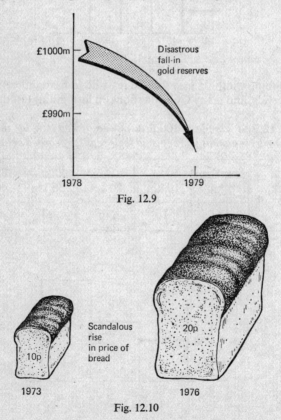

Fig. 12.9

Fig. 12.10

instead of lengths. In Fig. 12.10, the length of each loaf is proportional to the price, but the eye compares the volumes of the loaves.

Exercise 12c

1 In 1979 a certain company analysed its fixed assets in different regions of the world. 33% of its assets were in Great Britain, 27% of its assets were in Continental Europe, 25% in North America, and the rest were elsewhere. Draw a pie-chart (circular diagram) to display this data.

2 A case of apples was opened and each apple weighed. The distribution of mass of the apples is given by the table below:

Mass in grams	Number of apples
60–100	40
100–120	40
120–140	20
140–160	30
160–200	30

Draw a histogram to display this data.

13 Probability

Notes

Probability
The probability of an outcome A

$$= \frac{\text{number of } \textbf{equiprobable} \text{ favourable outcomes}}{\text{total number of equiprobable outcomes}},$$

If A and B denote two events,

$$\Pr(A \text{ or B or both}) = \Pr(A) + \Pr(B) - \Pr(\text{both } A \text{ and } B)$$

If A and B are two independent events,

$$\Pr(A \text{ and } B) = \Pr(A) \times \Pr(B)$$

Remember tree diagrams (p. 114) are often helpful.

Definition

We define the probability of an event as the ratio

$$\frac{\text{the number of equiprobable favourable outcomes}}{\text{total number of all equiprobable outcomes}}$$

e.g. Pr (a fair die shows a '6') $= \frac{1}{6}$, Pr (a card drawn at random from a well-shuffled pack is a heart) $= \frac{13}{52}$, if there is not a joker in the pack; the probability is $\frac{13}{54}$ if there are two jokers, as there are now 54 equiprobable outcomes, though still only 13 are 'favourable', **but** Pr (when two dice are thrown, both show 'heads') is **not** $\frac{1}{3}$ because the three outcomes '*two heads*', '*one head and one tail*', and '*two tails*' are not equiprobable. The equiprobable outcomes are H H, H T, T H, T T, so that the probability that both coins show heads is $\frac{1}{4}$. For many simple probability questions in Section A of GCE papers or in multiple-choice questions, it is sufficient to list all possible outcomes, and pick out those that are favourable.

Example 13.1 *A number is selected at random from the numbers integers 2 to 10 inclusive. Find the probability that the number chosen is (a) prime, (b) even, (c) a multiple of 3, (d) not a multiple of 3.*

The numbers integers from 2 to 10 inclusive are 2, 3, 4, 5, 6, 7, 8, 9, and 10, and they can be called the **possibility set**, $\mathscr{E}$, of all possible outcomes.

In (a), the subset A of favourable outcomes is 2, 3, 5, and 7. Thus the probability that a number drawn chosen at random is prime is $\frac{4}{9}, \frac{n\{A\}}{n\{\mathscr{E}\}}$.

In (b), the subset of favourable elements is 2, 4, 6, 8, and 10, so that Pr (number chosen at random is even) is $\frac{5}{9}$.

In (c), there are three multiples of three, 3, 6, and 9, so Pr (number chosen at random is a multiple of three) $= \frac{3}{9} = \frac{1}{3}$.

In (d), we can say that there are six numbers not multiples of three, so Pr (number chosen at random is not a multiple of three) $= \frac{6}{9} = \frac{2}{3}$, or we can say that either a number is a multiple of three or it is not a multiple of three, so that the probability that a number is a multiple of three is $1 - \frac{1}{3}$, i.e. $\frac{2}{3}$.

Exercise 13a

1 Four grey and three blue socks are in a laundry bag. If one is drawn at random, what is the probability that it is (a) grey, (b) blue?
2 x grey socks and y blue socks are in a laundry bag. If one is drawn at random, what is the probability that it is grey?
3 A letter is chosen at random from the letters LONDON. What is the probability that it is (a) L, (b) O?
4 A fair die has its faces marked 1, 1, 1, 2, 2, and 3. What is the probability that when thrown it shows a 1?
5 Assuming that a man is equally likely to be born on any day of the week, what is the probability that a man chosen at random was born on a Sunday?

Addition of probabilities

What is the probability that a card drawn at random from a pack of 52 cards is either a king or a heart? There are 52 cards to choose from; of these 13 are hearts, 4 are kings, but one is the king of hearts, and so has been counted twice. There are just 16 favourable different equiprobable draws we can make, so the probability that a card is a king or a heart is $\frac{16}{52}$, i.e. $\frac{4}{13}$.

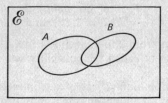

Fig. 13.1

The relation between the cards can be illustrated by the Venn diagram in Fig. 13.1, where $A = \{$all hearts$\}$ and $B = \{$all kings$\}$.

If $A \cup B$ is the set of all cards that are either hearts or kings or both, $A \cap B$ is the set of all cards that are both hearts and kings, i.e. the king of hearts, we have the rule

$$\text{Pr}(A \cup B) = \text{Pr}(A) + \text{Pr}(B) - \text{Pr}(A \cap B).$$

It may prove difficult to remember the rule in this form, but drawing a Venn diagram prevents any element being counted more than once.

Example 13.2 *Find the probability that a number chosen at random from the integers 2 to 10 inclusive is either a prime or a multiple of 3.*

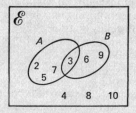

Fig. 13.2

If $A = \{$all primes$\}$, $B = \{$all multiples of 3$\}$, then the relation between the sets is illustrated in Fig. 13.2, and we see Pr (number is either a prime or a multiple of 3) $= \frac{6}{9}$, i.e. $\frac{2}{3}$.

Independent events

Two events which are such that one has no effect on the other are called independent events. We usually assume events are independent unless there is a clear connection between them, such as drawing a heart from a pack of cards at the second draw; this may depend on whether we have drawn a heart at the first draw.

Product rule

If we have two independent events A and B, then Pr (both A and B) = Pr $(A) \times$ Pr (B). This rule is illustrated in Examples 13.3 and 13.4.

Example 13.3 *A coin is thrown four times. Find the probability that it shows four heads.*

Pr (first throw shows heads) $= \frac{1}{2}$
Pr (second throw shows heads) $= \frac{1}{2}$
Pr (third throw shows heads) $= \frac{1}{2}$
and Pr (fourth throw shows heads) $= \frac{1}{2}$
so Pr (all four throws show heads) $= \frac{1}{2} \times \frac{1}{2} \times \frac{1}{2} \times \frac{1}{2} = \frac{1}{16}$

Example 13.4 *The probability that an athlete A breaks the record of a race is $\frac{1}{2}$; the probability that an athlete B breaks the record in the same race is $\frac{1}{3}$. Find the probability that (a) both will break the record, (b) neither breaks the record.*

It might be argued by athletes that these probabilities are dependent; that if A breaks the record, he will set a fast pace and so B might also break the record, but we have no information about the manner in which they are dependent, so assume that the probabilities are independent. Then

Pr (A breaks the record) $= \frac{1}{2}$
Pr (B breaks the record) $= \frac{1}{3}$
Pr (A and B break the record) $= \frac{1}{2} \times \frac{1}{3} = \frac{1}{6}$

Either A breaks the record or he does not break the record,

so that Pr (A does not break the record) $= 1 - \frac{1}{2} = \frac{1}{2}$
and Pr (B does not break the record) $= 1 - \frac{1}{3} = \frac{2}{3}$
therefore
Pr (neither A nor B breaks the record) $= \frac{1}{2} \times \frac{2}{3} = \frac{1}{3}$

In slightly more difficult examples it is helpful to draw a tree diagram.

Example 13.5 *A lecturer is supposed to give a course of four lectures; if he fails to give one, the lecture is given by his deputy. If the lecturer gives one lecture, the probability that he will not give the next is $\frac{3}{4}$; if he fails to give any one lecture, the probability that he will give the next is $\frac{2}{3}$. He is certain to give the first lecture. Find the probability that he (a) gives all four lectures; (b) gives the first and second but not the third; (c) gives the third lecture; (d) gives the fourth lecture.*

Draw a tree diagram, as Fig. 13.3. We do not need to put in all the probabilities to answer these four questions, but they are inserted

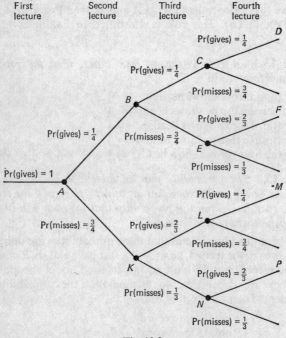

Fig. 13.3

here to show the probability of each event, and the ease with which many other questions on this data can be answered. The probability that he gives all four lectures is found by reading *A B C D*, i.e.

$$\text{Pr (gives all four lectures)} = 1 \times \tfrac{1}{4} \times \tfrac{1}{4} \times \tfrac{1}{4} = \tfrac{1}{64}$$

The probability that he gives the first and second lecture but not the third is found by reading $A\ B\ E$ (notice that we are not interested whether he gives the fourth lecture or not), so

Pr (he gives the first and second lectures but not the third)
$$= 1 \times \tfrac{1}{4} \times \tfrac{3}{4} = \tfrac{3}{16}$$

The probability that he gives the third lecture is found by reading $A\ B\ C$ and $A\ K\ L$.

$$\text{Pr (gives first, second, and third)} = 1 \times \tfrac{1}{4} \times \tfrac{1}{4} = \tfrac{1}{16}$$
$$\text{Pr (gives first, not second, gives third)} = 1 \times \tfrac{3}{4} \times \tfrac{2}{3} = \tfrac{1}{2}$$

For either of these sequence of events, he gives the third lecture, so

$$\text{Pr (he gives the third lecture)} = \tfrac{1}{16} + \tfrac{1}{2} = \tfrac{9}{16}$$

The probability that he gives the fourth lecture is found by reading along the paths $A\ B\ C\ D$, $A\ B\ E\ F$, $A\ K\ L\ M$, and $A\ K\ N\ P$. Thus

$$\text{Pr (gives the fourth lecture)} = \tfrac{1}{4} \times \tfrac{1}{4} + \tfrac{1}{4} + \tfrac{1}{4} \times \tfrac{3}{4} \times \tfrac{2}{3} + \tfrac{3}{4} \times \tfrac{2}{3} \times \tfrac{1}{4}$$
$$+ \tfrac{3}{4} \times \tfrac{1}{3} \times \tfrac{2}{3} = \tfrac{83}{192}$$

The working can be abbreviated by using $\tfrac{9}{16} \times \tfrac{1}{4} + \tfrac{7}{16} \times \tfrac{2}{3} = \tfrac{83}{192}$. Why?

Exercise 13b

1 A bag of sweets contains 7 toffees, 5 mints, and 3 chocolates, all wrapped identically. Sweets are drawn out one at a time and not replaced. Find the probability that

(a) the first drawn is a toffee;
(b) the first drawn is a toffee and the second a mint;
(c) the first and second drawn are both toffees;
(d) the second is a toffee;
(e) the third is a toffee;
(f) the fourth is a toffee.

Guess the probability that when six of the sweets have been drawn, the next is a toffee.

2 A certain boy either walks to school or cycles. If he walks one day, the probability that he cycles the next is $\tfrac{4}{5}$; if he cycles one day, the probability that he walks the next is $\tfrac{2}{3}$. He walks to school on Monday of one week. Find the probability that during one week he

(a) walks to school on both Tuesday and Wednesday;
(b) cycles on Tuesday and walks on Wednesday;
(c) walks on Wednesday;
(d) cycles on Wednesday;
(e) walks on Thursday;
(f) walks every day that week.

3 In a game of tennis, after the score 'deuce' has been reached, either one player wins both the next two points, and then he wins the game, or each player wins one of the two points, and the score of 'deuce' is called again. In a certain game between two players A and B, the probability that A wins any one point is 0.7. Given that the score of deuce has just been reached, find the probability that

(a) A wins the next two points (and hence the game);
(b) B wins the next two points (and hence the game);
(c) each player wins one point, and so the score of deuce is called a second time;
(d) the score of deuce is called a third time;
(e) that after the score deuce is called a third time, A wins the match.

14 Geometry: parallel lines, triangles, isometry, quadrilaterals

Notes on geometry

Some definitions
A triangle with no sides equal is called a **scalene** triangle.

A triangle with two (or more) sides equal is called an **isosceles** triangle.

A triangle with all three sides equal is called an **equilateral** triangle.

A quadrilateral with both pairs of opposite sides parallel is called a **parallelogram.**

A parallelogram with two adjacent sides equal is called a **rhombus.**

A parallelogram with one angle a right angle is called a **rectangle.**

A rectangle with adjacent sides equal is called a **square.**

Some properties of parallel lines
Corresponding angles and **alternate** angles are equal.

Adjacent angles are supplementary.

Some commonly-used theorems
1 The sum of the angles of a triangle is two right angles. (Corollary: the sum of the angles of an n-sided polygon is $(2n - 4)$ right angles.)
2 In any right-angled triangle, the square on the hypotenuse is equal to the sum of the squares on the other two sides (Pythagoras' Theorem).
3 The angle subtended by an arc of a circle at the centre is double the angle subtended by that arc at any other point on the remaining part of the circumference. (Corollaries: angles in the same segment

of a circle are equal; the opposite angles of a cyclic quadrilateral are supplementary; the angle in a semi-circle is a right angle.)

4 If two chords AB, CD of a circle intersect at a point X, $AX \cdot XB = CX \cdot XD$.

5 Equiangular triangles have their corresponding sides proportional.

Parallel lines, corresponding, alternate, and adjacent angles

In Fig. 14.1, AB is parallel to CD. Pairs of corresponding angles are a and c, h and b, g and e, f and d; corresponding angles are

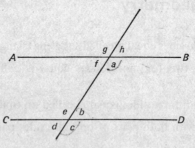

Fig. 14.1

equal. Pairs of alternate angles are f and b, a and e; alternate angles are *equal*. Pairs of adjacent angles are a and b, f and e; adjacent angles are *supplementary*, i.e. total 180°. Simple questions, some of them in multiple choice papers, are set testing only these properties.

Example 14.1 *In Fig.* 14.2, *PQ is parallel to TS. Which of the following statements is true?*

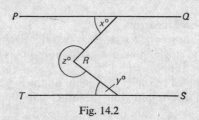

Fig. 14.2

(a) $x + y = z$ 　　　　(b) $x + y + z = 180$
(c) $x + y + z = 270$ 　(d) $x + y + z = 360$

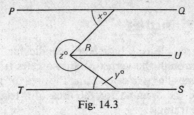

Fig. 14.3

Draw the line RU through R parallel to PQ. (This construction is often helpful.) Then angle $QRU = x°$ (alternate) and $SRU = y°$. These two angles, with angle $z°$, complete a full circle, so $x + y + z = 360$, the answer is (d).

Triangles, isosceles and equilateral

An isosceles triangle has a pair of sides equal in length; an equilateral triangle has three sides equal in length, so that all equilateral triangles are isosceles, a relation often tested in questions using Venn diagrams.

Example 14.2 *If $\mathscr{E} = \{all\ triangles\}$, $A = \{all\ isosceles\ triangles\}$, $B = \{all\ equilateral\ triangles\}$, $C = \{all\ right-angled\ triangles\}$, draw a Venn diagram illustrating the relation between the sets. Show that all elements of the set $A \cap C$ are similar, and that $B \cap C = \emptyset$.*

The relation between the sets is illustrated by the Venn diagram in Fig. 14.4. Since all triangles in the set $A \cap C$ are isosceles and right-

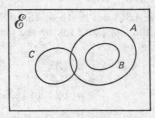

Fig. 14.4

angled, the angle sizes must be 45°, 45°, 90°, so the triangles are similar. Since all equilateral triangles have all angles equal to 60°, no equilateral triangle contains a right angle,

$$B \cap C = \emptyset$$

Areas of triangles

The area of a triangle is $\frac{1}{2}$ base × perpendicular height. Since the perpendicular through the vertex of an isosceles triangle bisects the base this sometimes helps in calculating the area of isosceles triangles. We can also use the formula for the area of a triangle to calculate the height of the triangle.

Example 14.3 *In the isosceles triangle ABC, AB = AC = 17 cm and BC = 16 cm. Calculate the area of the triangle, and hence the perpendicular distance of B from AC.*

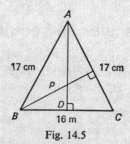

Fig. 14.5

Draw the perpendicular bisector of *BC*, to meet *BC* in *D*. Then by Pythagoras' theorem, $AB^2 = AD^2 + BD^2$

$$\text{i.e. } AD^2 = 17^2 - 8^2$$
$$= 225$$
$$AD = 15$$

so the area of triangle *ABC* = $\frac{1}{2}$ × 16 × 15, i.e. 120 cm².

Regarding *AC* as the base, and taking the perpendicular distance of *B* from *AC* as *p* (Fig. 14.5),

$$\frac{1}{2} \times 17 \times p = 120,$$
$$p = \tfrac{240}{17},$$
$$= 14.1, \text{ to 3 s.f.}$$

The perpendicular distance of B from AC is about 14.1 cm.

Exercise 14a

1 In Fig. 14.6, *AB* is parallel to *PQ*. Copy the following statements, and complete each, using one of the words *alternate, corresponding, supplementary*.

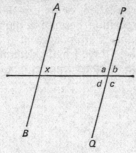

Fig. 14.6

(a) Angles x and a are . . .
(b) Angles x and b are . . .
(c) Angles x and c are . . .
(d) Angles x and d are . . .

2 In Fig. 14.7 AB is parallel to PQ. If AX and PX are the angle bisectors, prove that $A\widehat{X}P = 90°$.

3 One angle of an isosceles triangle is twice another angle. Find the sizes of the angles in the triangle.

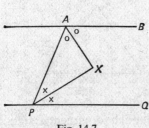

Fig. 14.7

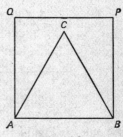

Fig. 14.8

4 In the triangle ABC, $AB = 8$ cm, $BC = 9$ cm, and $ABC = 90°$. Find the area of the triangle, and hence the perpendicular distance of B from AC.

5 In Fig. 14.8, an equilateral triangle ABC is inscribed in a square $ABPQ$. Calculate the angle BCP.

Congruent triangles

Two triangles are congruent if one can be superimposed on to the other. We can think of this 'placing on top' being done by reflection by rotation, or by translation, or we can show that it is possible to carry out the superposition because certain sides and angles are equal. Thus two triangles are congruent if $AB = XY$, $BC = YZ$, and $CA = ZX$, as these three lengths determine a triangle uniquely (Fig. 14.9). This case of congruence is denoted by SSS (side, side,

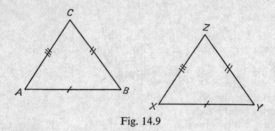

Fig. 14.9

side). In Fig. 14.10, the triangles will be congruent if $AB = XY$ $BC = YZ$ and angle $ABC =$ angle XYZ. Again, a triangle is uniquely determined. This case of congruence is denoted SAS (side, included

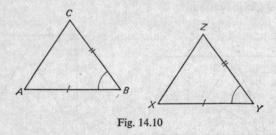

Fig. 14.10

angle, side). In Fig. 14.11, the triangles will be congruent if $AB = XY$, angle $CAB =$ angle ZXY, angle $XYZ =$ angle ABC. This case is abbreviated ASA (angle, side, angle). The final case of congruency

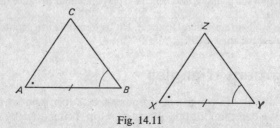

Fig. 14.11

is illustrated in Fig. 14.12, where the triangles have two pairs of sides equal, and one angle of each triangle is a right angle. Notice (Fig. 14.13) that two triangles are not congruent if two pairs of

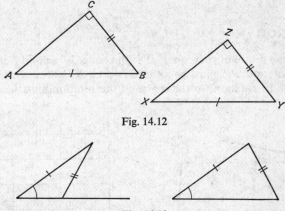

Fig. 14.12

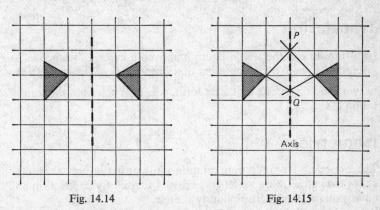

Fig. 14.13

sides are equal and a pair of not-included angles are equal, for two different triangles could be constructed from that data.

Reflection

If one figure is reflected in a certain straight line to give another figure, the straight line is called the **axis of reflection**. To find the axis, take

Fig. 14.14   Fig. 14.15

any straight line in one figure, and its image in the other figure. Produce both until they meet in a point P. Select another straight line and its image, and produce them until they meet in a point Q. Then the line PQ will be the axis of reflection.

Rotation

To find the centre of rotation, if P' is the image of a point P under a certain rotation, PP' must be a chord of a circle, whose centre is the centre of the rotation, so the centre of the rotation must lie on the

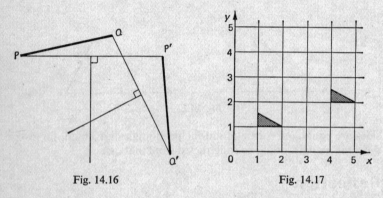

Fig. 14.16   Fig. 14.17

perpendicular bisector of PP'. Similarly, if Q' is the image of a point Q, the centre lies on the perpendicular bisector of QQ'.

Translation

In a translation, the whole figure is moved a certain distance in a given direction. We may be given the components of the translation in two fixed directions in matrix form, e.g., $\begin{pmatrix} 3 \\ 1 \end{pmatrix}$ describes the translation in Fig. 14.17.

Isometries

These operations of reflection, rotation, and translation are sometimes called isometries, because lengths are not altered. By contrast, in an enlargement, lengths are obviously altered.

Example 14.4 *In Fig.* 14.18, *AB = AD, AC = AE and BC = DE.*
Prove that triangles BAE, DAC are congruent.

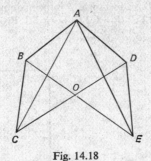

Fig. 14.18

In triangles ABC, ADE,

$$AB = AD \text{ (given)}$$
$$BC = DE \text{ (given)}$$
$$AC = AE \text{ (given)}$$

∴ triangles ABC, ADE are congruent (SSS).
Since these triangles are congruent,

$$\text{angle } BAC = \text{angle } DAE$$

Adding angle CAE to each,

$$\text{angle } BAE = \text{angle } CAD.$$

In triangles BAE, DAC,

$$AB = AD \text{ (given)}$$
$$\text{angle } BAE = \text{angle } CAD \text{ (proved)}$$
$$AE = AC \text{ (given)}$$

Therefore triangles BAE, DAC are congruent (SAS).

Alternatively, we can show that AO is the axis of symmetry of the
figure, and that triangle BAE reflects in AO to give triangle DAC.

Exercise 14b

1 In Fig. 14.19, $ABCD$ is part of a regular twenty-sided polygon.
  Prove that $AC = BD$ by (a) using congruent triangles, (b) by finding
  the centre of a certain rotation.

2 In an isosceles triangle ABC, X is the midpoint of AB and Y the midpoint of AC. Prove that $CX = BY$ by (a) using congruent triangles, (b) using a certain reflection.

3 In Fig. 14.20 $ABCD$ is a rectangle. P is the midpoint of BC, Q the midpoint of AD; $AX:XB = CY:YD = 2:1$. Prove, by two methods, that $XP = QY$.

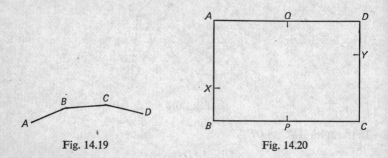

Fig. 14.19   Fig. 14.20

Quadrilaterals

Parallelogram

A parallelogram is defined as a quadrilateral with both pairs of opposite sides parallel. From this definition we can prove

1 both pairs of opposite sides are equal;
2 both pairs of opposite angles are equal;
3 the diagonals bisect each other.

It is a useful exercise in congruent triangles, and in the symmetry of the figure, to prove these.

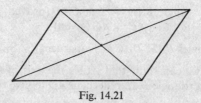

Fig. 14.21

N.B. A parallelogram has rotational symmetry about the intersection of the diagonals, and is *not* symmetrical about a diagonal, unless it is a rhombus.

Rhombus

A parallelogram with one pair of adjacent sides equal is called a rhombus. It can be proved, and again is a useful exercise in congruent triangles or the symmetry of the figure, that

1 all sides of a rhombus are equal;
2 the diagonals of a rhombus bisect each other at right angles;
3 each diagonal of a rhombus bisects the angles through which it passes.

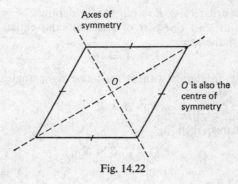

Fig. 14.22

Rectangle

A parallelogram with one angle a right angle is called a rectangle. It can be proved that

(a) all angles of a rectangle are right angles;
(b) the diagonals of a rectangle are equal.

Square

A rectangle with two adjacent sides equal is called a square. A square has all the properties of the parallelogram, rhombus, and rectangle.

Kite

A quadrilateral with two pairs of adjacent sides equal is called a kite. A kite has one axis of symmetry, and its diagonals meet at right angles. The relation between these types of quadrilaterals is illustrated in Fig. 14.23.

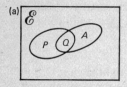 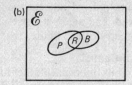 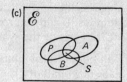

Fig. 14.23

If $\mathscr{E}$ = {all quadrilaterals}, P = {all parallelograms}, A = {all quadrilaterals with at least one pair of adjacent sides equal} and Q = {all rhombuses}, then

$$P \cap A = Q$$

If B = {all quadrilaterals with at least one right angle} and R = {all rectangles}, then

$$P \cap B = R$$

If S = {all squares}, then

$$P \cap A \cap B = S$$

Exercise 14c

1 If K = {all kites}, P = {all parallelograms}, and R = {all rhombuses}, draw a Venn diagram to illustrate the relation between the sets K, P, and R.

2 If $\mathscr{E}$ = {all quadrilaterals}, P = {all parallelograms}, R = {all rectangles}, S = {all squares}, T = {all trapezia},† V = {all rhombuses}, which of the following are true?

(a) $S \subset R$ (b) $V \subset P$
(c) $R \subset P$ (d) $P' \subset R'$
(e) $P \subset T$ (f) $T' \subset S'$

† A trapezium is a quadrilateral with one pair of opposite sides parallel.

15 Commonly-used theorems

The sum of the angles in a triangle

By drawing the straight line through B parallel to AC, we can prove that (a) the exterior angle of a triangle is equal to the sum of the two interior opposite angles, and (b) the sum of the angles of the triangle ABC is 180° (Fig 15.1).

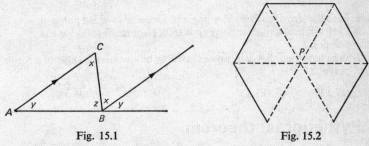

Fig. 15.1   Fig. 15.2

The sum of the angles of an n-sided polygon

By choosing a suitable point P inside the polygon, we can construct n triangles. The sum of the angles in these triangles is $2n$ right angles. But there are 4 right angles at the point P, so that the sum of the angles of the polygon is $(2n - 4)$ right angles (Fig 15.2).

Regular polygons

A regular polygon has all sides equal and all angles equal. Thus each angle of a regular polygon has $\frac{1}{n}(2n - 4)$ degrees (Fig 15.3). It is usually easier to calculate the exterior angle of a regular polygon, then find the interior one by subtraction from 180°.

Example 15.1 *Find the interior angle of a regular twelve-sided polygon.*

Since the exterior angles total 360°, each will be $\frac{1}{12} \times 360°$ i.e. 30° (Fig 15:4), so that the interior angles will be 150°.

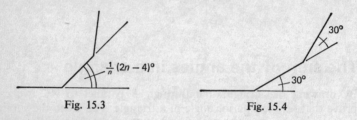

Fig. 15.3   Fig. 15.4

Exercise 15a

1 Find the size of each interior angle of a regular 15-sided polygon.
2 Each angle of a regular polygon is 162°. How many sides has the polygon?
3 Which of the following can not possibly be an exterior angle of a regular polygon?

(a) 12°   (b) 15°   (c) 16°   (d) 18°

Pythagoras' theorem

In a right-angled triangle, the square on the hypotenuse is equal to the sum of the squares on the other two sides. When applying this theorem, always write down the square on the hypotenuse first, then the squares on the other two sides.

Converse

It is sometimes necessary to distinguish between a theorem and its converse. The converse of Pythagoras' theorem illustrates this distinction. The converse is that if in a triangle, the square on one side is equal to the sum of the squares on the other two sides, then the angle opposite the longest side is a right angle.

This can be extended to show that, if in a triangle the square on one side is greater than the sum of the squares on the other two sides, then the angle opposite the longest side is greater than a right angle. A similar result holds if the relation is 'less than'.

Example 15.2   *In the triangle ABC, AD = 6 cm, BD = 4 cm and DC = 9 cm. AD is perpendicular to BC. Prove that angle BAC is a right angle.*

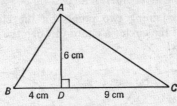

Fig. 15.5

Since $B\widehat{D}A = 90°$, $AB^2 = BD^2 + DA^2$ (Pythagoras' theorem)

$$= 4^2 + 6^2$$
$$= 52$$

Since $A\widehat{D}C = 90°$, $AC^2 = AD^2 + DC^2$ (Pythagoras' theorem)

$$= 6^2 + 9^2$$
$$= 117$$

In triangle ABC,

$$AB^2 + AC^2 = 52 + 117$$
$$= 169$$
$$= 13^2$$
$$= BC^2,$$

Therefore angle BAC is a right angle (converse of Pythagoras' theorem).

Exercise 15b

1 In the triangle ABC, angle $ABC = 90°$, $AB = 7$ cm, and $BC = 24$ cm. Calculate the length of AC.
2 In the right-angled triangle ABC, $AB = 8$ cm and $BC = 15$ cm. Find the two possible lengths for AC.
3 In triangle ABC, $AB = 11$ cm, $BC = 13$ cm, and $AC = 17$ cm. Is angle ABC greater than, equal to, or less than a right angle?
4 Show that, for all values of m, any triangle whose sides are in the ratio $(m^2 + 1) : 2m : (m^2 - 1)$ is right-angled.
5 In the triangle ABC, angle $ABC = 90°$. If M is the midpoint of AC, show that $AB^2 + BC^2 = 2AM^2 + 2BM^2$. (Hint: draw BN perpendicular to AC to meet AC at N.)

Circle theorems

A point in a plane whose distance from a fixed point in that plane is constant lies on the circumference of a **circle**; the length of the circumference of a circle radius r is $2\pi r$; the area enclosed by the circle is πr^2.

A straight line joining two points on the circumference of a circle is a **chord** of the circle; a chord through the centre of a circle is called a **diameter**.

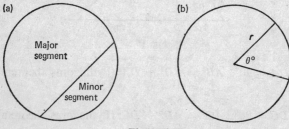

Fig. 15.6

A chord cuts a circle into two **segments** (Fig. 15.6a). Two radii determine a **sector** of a circle (Fig. 15.6b). If the angle between the radii is $\theta°$, the length of the arc is $\dfrac{\theta}{360} \times 2\pi r$, and the area of the sector is $\dfrac{\theta}{360} \times \pi r^2$.

From the definition of the circle it follows that we have many isosceles triangles, which can be used in calculations and proofs on the circle. A circle is also symmetrical about every line through its centre.

The angle which an arc of a circle subtends at the centre of a circle is twice that subtended by the arc at any other point on the circumference of the circle.

Fig. 15.7 illustrates the three possible cases. The theorem follows immediately from the definition, triangles OAP, OBP being isosceles, and the exterior angle of a triangle being equal to the sum of the two interior angles. There are several important corollaries to this theorem.

1 Angles in the same segment of a circle are equal (Fig. 15.8a)

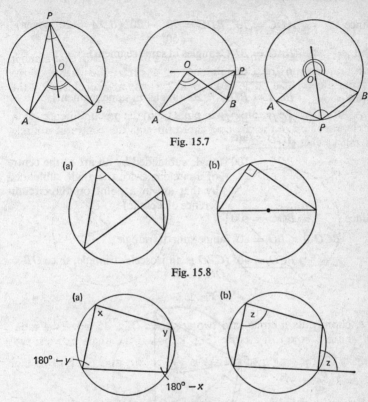

Fig. 15.7

(a)   (b)

Fig. 15.8

(a)   (b)

Fig. 15.9

2 The angle in a semicircle is a right angle (Fig. 15.8b).
3 The opposite angles of a cyclic quadrilateral are supplementary (Fig. 15.9a), and hence the exterior angle of a cyclic quadrilateral is equal to the interior opposite angle. (Fig. 15.9b).

These should be known thoroughly, as they are tested regularly in those examinations in which they are part of the syllabus.

Example 15.3 *In Fig. 15.10, angle $ABC = 110°$, $BCD = 60°$, angle $BDA = 20°$. Calculate the angles ADC, BAC, ACD, BOC, and CBO.*

$$\widehat{ADC} = 180° - 110° \text{ (opposite angles of a cyclic quad-}$$
$$\text{rilateral are supplementary.)}$$
$$\therefore \underline{\widehat{ADC} = 70°}.$$

Since $\qquad A\widehat{D}C = 70°, B\widehat{D}C = 70° - 20° (B\widehat{D}A = 20°, \text{given})$
$\qquad\qquad\qquad\qquad = 50°$

But $\qquad B\widehat{A}C = B\widehat{D}C$ (angles in same segment)

$\therefore \underline{B\widehat{A}C = 50°}$

Now $\qquad B\widehat{C}A = B\widehat{D}A = 20°$ (angles in same segment)

$\therefore A\widehat{C}D = B\widehat{C}D - B\widehat{D}A = 60° - 20°$

$\therefore \underline{A\widehat{C}D = 40°}$

$\qquad\quad \underline{B\widehat{O}C = 100°}$ (angle subtended by an arc at the centre
of a circle is twice the angle subtended
by that arc at a point on the circumference of a circle)

Since $\qquad B\widehat{O}C = 100°$

$\quad B\widehat{C}O + C\widehat{B}O = 80°$ (angle sum of triangle)

$\therefore \underline{B\widehat{C}O = 40°}$ (CBO is an isosceles triangle, since $OB = OC$, radii)

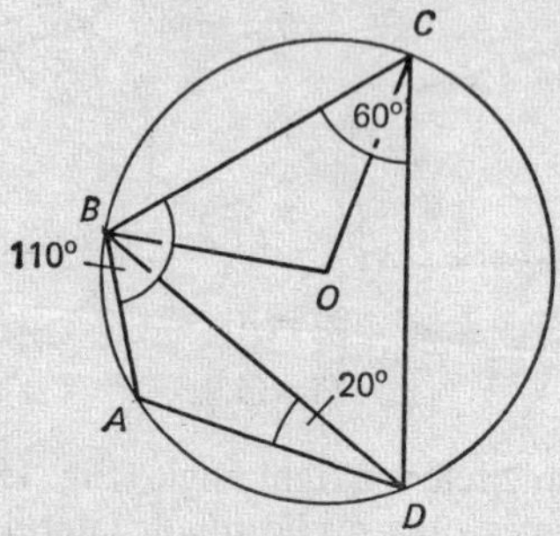

Fig. 15.10

Example 15.4 *Two circles intersect in points C and D, as in Fig. 15.11. BCY and ADX are straight lines. Prove that AB is parallel to XY.*

In the cyclic quadrilateral $ABCD$, $A\widehat{B}C = C\widehat{D}X$ (exterior angle of a cyclic quadrilateral is equal to the interior opposite angle).

In the cyclic quadrilateral $CDXY$, $C\widehat{D}X + X\widehat{Y}C = 180°$ (opposite angles of a cyclic quadrilateral are supplementary).

∴ $\widehat{ABC}$ and $\widehat{CYX}$ are supplementary,

∴ AB is parallel to XY ($\widehat{ABC}$, $\widehat{CYX}$ adjacent angles).

N.B. Always be perfectly clear about the reason for any statement or calculation. Do not confuse *equal* angles with *supplementary* angles.

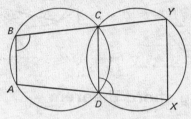

Fig. 15.11

Tangents

A tangent to a circle is perpendicular to the radius through the point of contact. Two tangents drawn from a point P to a circle are

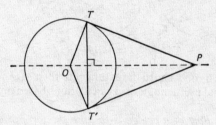

Fig. 15.12

equal in length, and Fig. 15.12 is symmetrical about the line OP. From this we can deduce that TT' is perpendicular to OP.

Alternate segment theorem

The angle between a tangent and the chord through the point of contact is equal to the angle in the alternate segment. There are two angles between the tangent and the chord and two segments (Fig. 15.13).

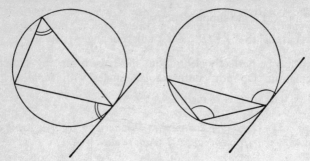

Fig. 15.13

Intersecting chord theorem

If AB and CD are two chords of a circle intersecting at a point O, either inside or outside the circle, then $AO \times OB = CO \times OD$.

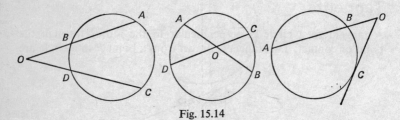

Fig. 15.14

In particular, if one chord is a tangent, then $AO \times OB = CO^2$. There are several useful numerical calculations based on this theorem.

Example 15.5 *Part of a bridge is to take the form of a circular arc, with a span of 40 m. The highest point of this arc is to be 10 m above the chord through the ends of the arc. Find the radius of the circular arc.*

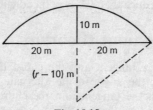

Fig. 15.15

With the notation in Fig. 15.15, $AO \times OB = CO \times OD$ (intersecting chord theorem). If the radius of the circle is r metres,

$$20 \times 20 = 10 \times (2r - 10)$$
$$2r - 10 = 40$$
$$r = 25$$

Therefore the radius is 25 metres.

Example 15.6   *Find the distance to the horizon from a point on a balloon drifting over an ocean, 200 m above sea-level.*

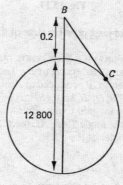

Fig. 15.16

Taking the Earth to be a sphere 6400 km radius, and using Fig. 15.16 (not drawn to scale),

$$BC^2 = 0.2 \times 12800.2$$

(We can use 12 800 without much loss of accuracy.)

$$BC^2 = 2560,$$
$$BC = 50.6, \text{ to 3 s.f.}$$

Therefore the distance to the horizon is about 50.6 km.

Exercise 15c

1 In Fig. 15.17(a), angle $ABC = 38°$. Calculate angles AOC, ACO, ACT.
2 In Fig. 15.17(b) angle ABC is 40°. Calculate angles AOC, ACO, ADC, ACT, and ACS.
3 If instead, in Fig. 15.17(b), angle ABC is known to be between 40° and

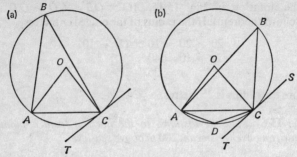

Fig. 15.17

46°, find the greatest and least possible sizes of the angles AOC and OCA

4 A, B, and C are three points on a circle centre O. Angles AOB, BOC, and AOC are 70°, 50°, and 120° respectively. The straight line through O perpendicular to AB meets CB produced at P and meets AC at S. Calculate the angles ACB, OPB, and ASP.

5 In Fig. 15.18, TAS is the tangent to the circle at A. AB is any chord through A, AK bisects the angle TAB, AL bisects the angle BAS. Prove that KL is a diameter of the circle.

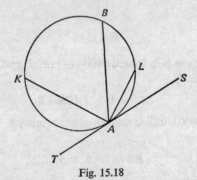

Fig. 15.18

Similar triangles

Equiangular triangles have corresponding sides proportional.

Using Fig. 15.19,

$$\frac{AB}{XY} = \frac{BC}{YZ} = \frac{CA}{ZX}$$

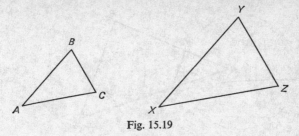

Fig. 15.19

The converse of this theorem is also true, that if corresponding sides are proportional, then the triangles are equiangular.

Enlargement

If the triangles are suitably situated, it is possible to describe one triangle as an enlargement of the other. In Fig. 15.20 $\frac{AB}{XY} = \frac{BC}{YZ} = \frac{AC}{XZ}$ $= \frac{1}{3}$; triangle ABC has been enlarged, centre O, by a factor of 3. Notice that the ratio $OA:OX$, etc is also $1:3$, whereas A divides OX

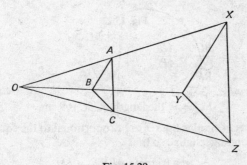

Fig. 15.20

in the ratio $1:2$. Take particular care in using given ratios correctly; this is a common source of error.

Example 15.7 *In triangle ABC (Fig 15.21), PQ is parallel to BC. $AB = 6$ cm, $PQ = 3$ cm, and $AP:PB = 1:2$. Calculate (a) the length of BC, (b) the ratio of the area triangle APQ : triangle ABC.*

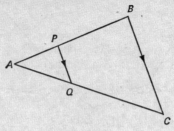

Fig. 15.21

(a) Since PQ is parallel to BC, triangles APQ and ABC are equi-angular, so corresponding sides are proportional. It is often helpful to separate the triangles.

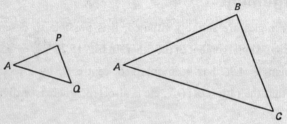

Fig. 15.22

$$\frac{BC}{PQ} = \frac{AB}{AP}$$
$$\therefore \quad \frac{BC}{3} = \frac{6}{2}$$
$$\therefore \quad BC = 9, \text{ the length of } BC \text{ is 9 cm.}$$

(b) The areas of similar figures are proportional to the squares of the corresponding lengths, so that

$$\frac{\text{area triangle } APQ}{\text{area triangle } ABC} = \left(\frac{1}{3}\right)^2$$

and the ratio of the areas is $1:9$.

Remember that the ratio of corresponding volumes of similar solids is the cube of the ratio of corresponding lengths.

Exercise 15d

1 A straight line parallel to the base BC of the triangle ABC meets AB in X and AC in Y. If $AX:XB = 3:4$, find the ratios (a) $AY:YC$, (b) $XY:BC$.

2 In the parallelogram $ABCD$, H and K are the points in AD and BC respectively such that $AH:HD = 2:1$ and $BK:KC = 1:3$. Lines through H and K parallel to AB meet AC in X and Y respectively. Find the ratios (a) $AX:XC$, (b) $AY:YC$, (c) $AY:YX$, (d) $YX:XC$.

3 In the square $ABCD$, E and F are points in AB, BC respectively such that $AE:EB = 1:2$ and $BF:FC = 1:2$. The lines AF and DE meet at X. Prove that the triangles AEX, AFB are similar, and that their areas are in the ratio $1:10$.

4 A straight tunnel is bored through the Earth, assumed to be a sphere radius 6400 km.

  (a) If the tunnel is 4000 km long, how near does it pass to the centre of the Earth?

  (b) If the tunnel is to pass through a point 2000 km from the centre of the Earth, what is the length of the tunnel?

5

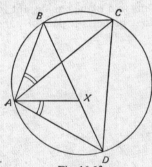

Fig. 15.23

In Fig. 15.23, angle $DAX = $ angle BAC.

  (a) Prove that triangles ABC, AXD are similar.

  (b) Prove that $AD.BC = AC.XD$.

  (c) Prove that triangles AXB, ADC are similar.

  (d) Prove that $AB.CD = AC.XB$.

  (e) From (b) and (d), deduce Ptolemy's theorem

$$AD.BC + AB.CD = AC.BD.$$

16 Loci and constructions

Locus

A **locus** is a set of points satisfying a given condition. This can be used to define a certain curve, as when a circle is defined as the set of all points equidistant from a fixed point. Some common loci are as follows:

1 The set of all points in a plane equidistant from a fixed point is a circle.
2 The set of all points in space equidistant from a fixed point is a sphere.
3 The set of all points in a plane equidistant from a fixed (infinite) straight line in that plane is a pair of parallel infinite straight lines (Fig 16.1).

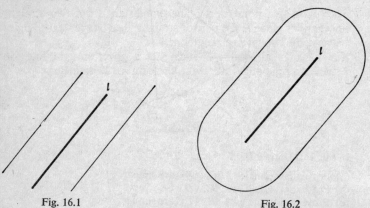

Fig. 16.1   Fig. 16.2

4 The set of all points in a plane distant d from a fixed (infinite) straight line not in that plane is also a pair of parallel straight lines, but not $2d$ apart.

In (3) and (4), if we have a finite straight line segment *l*, then we have to consider the end points separately. The locus of a point a given distance *d* from some one point in a line-segment *l* consists of a pair of straight lines joined by two semi-circular arcs (Fig. 16.2).

5 The locus in space of a point a fixed distance from a fixed (infinite) straight line is a circular cylinder. Again, if we have a line-segment, the locus becomes a cylinder with spherical ends.

6 The locus of a point in a plane equidistant from two fixed points *A*, *B* is the perpendicular bisector (sometimes called the mediator) of the straight line joining *A* and *B*.

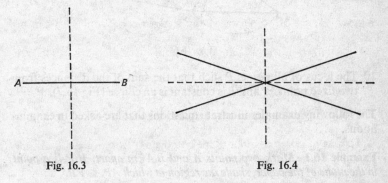

Fig. 16.3   Fig. 16.4

7 The locus of a point in a plane equidistant from two straight lines in that plane is the pair of straight lines bisecting the angles between the two given straight lines.

8 The locus of all points *P* such that a given straight line *AB* subtends a right angle at *P* is the circle on *AB* as diameter.

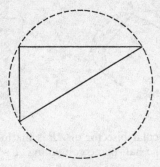

Fig. 16.5

9 Constant angle locus. The locus of all points P such that a given line-segment AB subtends a constant angle x at P is an arc of a circle through A and B. Strictly, the locus is the arcs of two circles through A and B.

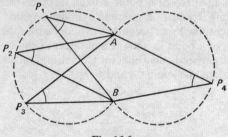

Fig. 16.6

10 The locus of all points P such that the sum of the distances from two fixed points A and B is constant is an ellipse (Fig 16.7).

The following examples illustrate questions that are asked in examinations.

Example 16.1 *Mark two points A and B 4 cm apart. If P is a point in the plane of the paper, shade the region in which $AP < PB$.*

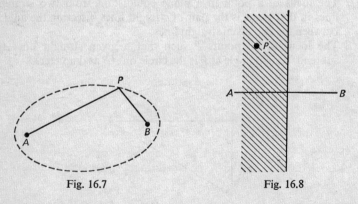

Fig. 16.7   Fig. 16.8

Since the perpendicular bisector of AB is the locus of all points for which $AP = PB$, the half-plane containing A will be the region for which $AP < PB$.

Example 16.2 *Mark two points A and B 6 cm apart. If P is a point in the plane of the paper, shade the outer boundary of the region in which* $\widehat{APB} > 50°$.

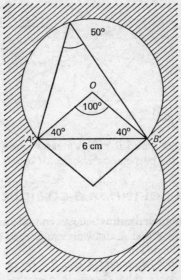

Fig. 16.9

To construct the boundary of the region accurately, we need to find the centres of the two circles. Since the angle at the circumference is 50°, the angle at the centre will be 100°, so each angle made by a radius with AB will be 40°. Using protractors we can find the two centres, and the radius OA; we can then draw the two circular arcs. The outer boundary of the region enclosed by those arcs we shade as required.

Example 16.3 *Two points A and B are 5 cm apart. Find the locus of the point P such that the area of the triangle APB is 10 cm².*

Since the area of a triangle is $\frac{1}{2}$ base × perpendicular height, the vertex P must lie on one of the two straight lines 4 cm from AB (Fig 16.10).

Some useful constructions

To draw the perpendicular bisector (mediator) of the straight line segment AB (Fig 16.11).

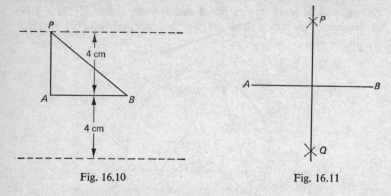

Fig. 16.10   Fig. 16.11

Draw arcs, centres *A* and *B*, radius greater than $\frac{1}{2}$ *AB*. If they meet in *P* and *Q*, *PQ* is the perpendicular bisector of *AB*.

To reflect a point *P* in a straight line *l*

Draw an arc of a circle, radius *r* large enough to cut *l*, to meet *l* in *A* and *B*. Centres *A* and *B*, draw arcs radii *r*, to cut at *Q*. Then *Q* is the image of *P* reflected in *l*.

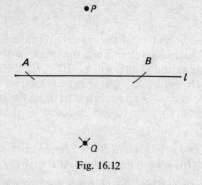

Fig. 16.12

To reflect a given straight line *m* in a given straight line *l*

If *l* and *m* intersect on the paper, call the point of intersection *R*. Reflect any one point *P* in the line *l*. If *Q* is the image in *l* of any one point *P* in the line *m*, then *QR* is the image of *m*.

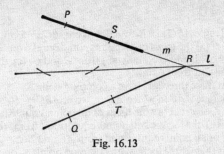

Fig. 16.13

If *l* and *m* do not meet on the paper, find the images *Q* and *T* of any two points *P* and *S* in *l*. Then *QT* is the image of *m*.

To find the centre of a rotation

If *P'* is the image of a point *P* and *Q'* is the image of a point *Q*, the centre *O* of the rotation is the intersection of the perpendicular bisectors of *PP'* and *QQ'* (Fig 16.14).

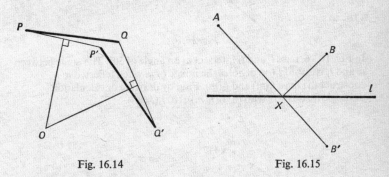

Fig. 16.14   Fig. 16.15

To draw the shortest path from a point *A* to another point *B*, going through some one point in a straight line *l* not through *A* or *B*

If *B'* is the image in *l* of *B*, join *AB'*. If this meets *l* in *X*, *AXB* is the shortest route Fig 16.15.

Exercise 16

1 Draw the triangle ABC in which $AB = 4$ cm, $BC = 5$ cm, and $CA = 6$ cm. Construct (a) the locus of all points equidistant from A and B; (b) the locus of all points equidistant from B and C; (c) the locus of all points equidistant from C and A.
  Verify that these three loci have a common point.

2 Draw the triangle ABC in which $AB = 6$ cm, $ABC = 50°$, and $CAB = 60°$. Construct (a) the locus of all points equidistant from AB and BC; (b) the locus of all points equidistant from AC and AB; (c) the locus of all points equidistant from AC and BC.
  Verify that these three loci have a common point.

3

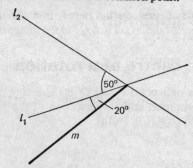

Fig. 16.16

In Fig. 16.16, lines l_1 and l_2 intersect at an angle of 50°. The angle between m and l_1 is 20°. If $l_1(m)$ denotes the image of m when reflected in l_1, construct the lines $l_1(m)$ and $l_2(m)$. Find by drawing or calculation the angle made by m with (a) $l_2(l_1(m))$, (b) $l_1(l_2(m))$.

4

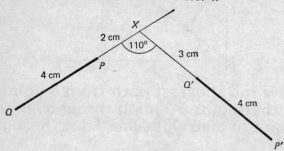

Fig. 16.17

In Fig. 16.17, $PQ = P'Q' = 4$ cm, $PX = 2$ cm, $Q'X = 3$ cm, and angle $Q'XP = 110°$. Construct the centre of the rotation which has transformed PQ into $P'Q'$, and measure the angle of rotation.

17 Trigonometry: definitions, right-angled triangles

Notes on trigonometry

The ratios

$$\sin \text{ is } \frac{\text{opposite}}{\text{hypotenuse}}, \text{ or the projection onto } Oy$$

$$\cos \text{ is } \frac{\text{adjacent}}{\text{hypotenuse}}, \text{ or the projection onto } Ox$$

$$\tan \text{ is } \frac{\text{opposite}}{\text{adjacent}}, \text{ or } \frac{\sin}{\cos}$$

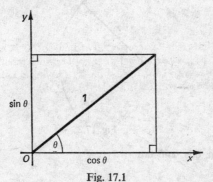

Fig. 17.1

$$\cot \text{ is } \frac{1}{\tan}; \sec \text{ is } \frac{1}{\cos}; \csc \text{ is } \frac{1}{\sin}$$

Some useful results

$$\sin \ 0° = \cos 90° = 0$$
$$\sin 30° = \cos 60° = \tfrac{1}{2}$$
$$\sin 45° = \cos 45° = \frac{1}{\sqrt{2}}$$

$$\sin 60° = \cos 30° = \tfrac{1}{2}\sqrt{3}$$
$$\sin 90° = \cos \ 0° = 1$$
$$\sin^2 A + \cos^2 A = 1, \text{ for all angles } A.$$

Sine formula

$$\frac{a}{\sin A} = \frac{b}{\sin B} = \frac{c}{\sin C} = 2R$$

Cosine formula

$$a^2 = b^2 + c^2 - 2bc \cos A,$$

i.e. $$\cos A = \frac{b^2 + c^2 - a^2}{2bc}$$

Area of a triangle
$$\triangle = \tfrac{1}{2}bc \sin A = \sqrt{\{s(s-a)(s-b)(s-c)\}}, \text{ where } s = \tfrac{1}{2}(a+b+c)$$

Arc and sector

Length of an arc is $\dfrac{\theta}{360} (2\pi r)$

Area of a sector is $\dfrac{\theta}{360} (\pi r^2)$

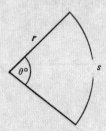

Fig. 17.2

Graphs of sin, cos, and tan

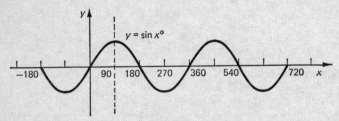

Fig. 17.3

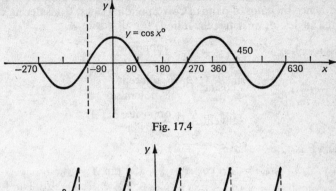

Fig. 17.4

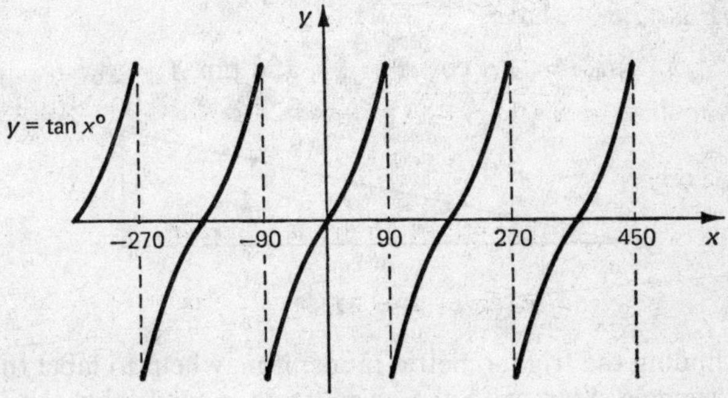

Fig. 17.5

Definitions

Equiangular triangles have corresponding sides proportional, so if one angle in each triangle is known to be a right angle, then when a

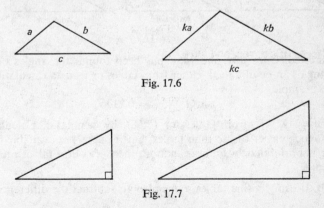

Fig. 17.6

Fig. 17.7

second angle is given, the three angles of the triangle are determined, and hence the ratio of pairs of corresponding sides. Considering one of the angles, A, we define the ratios

$$\text{sine } A = \frac{\text{opposite}}{\text{hypotenuse}}$$

$$\text{cosine } A = \frac{\text{adjacent}}{\text{hypotenuse}}$$

and
$$\text{tangent } A = \frac{\text{opposite}}{\text{adjacent}}$$

Using Fig. 17.8, we have

$$\sin A = \tfrac{9}{41}, \cos A = \tfrac{40}{41}, \text{ and } \tan A = \tfrac{9}{40}.$$

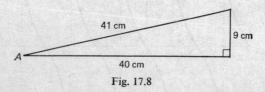

Fig. 17.8

When finding the trigonometric ratios, it may help to label the sides of the triangle. Start with the given angle A, and label the longest side the hypotenuse; the side next to the angle is the adjacent side, then the third side is that opposite the angle in which we are

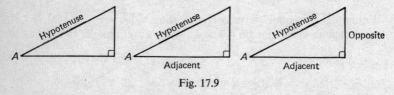

Fig. 17.9

interested. Once any one ratio has been found, the angles of the triangle can be obtained, either from tables or using a calculator. In this example,

$$\sin A = \tfrac{9}{41} = 0.2195$$

$\therefore A = 12° \, 41'$, from tables, or $12.68°$, by calculator. Calculators are much easier to use than tables, but if one is not available or its use is prohibited in an examination, then of course tables must be used.

N.B. If using cosine tables, remember to subtract the difference.

Example 17.1 *Find (a)* cos 38° 40' *(b) the angle whose cosine is* 0.8600.
(a) From the tables,

$$\cos 38° 36' = 0.7815$$
$$\text{the difference for } 4' = 7$$

$$\therefore \qquad \cos 38° 40' = 0.7808$$

(b) From tables,

$$0.8607 = \cos 30° 36'$$
$$7 = \text{the difference for } 5'$$
$$0.8600 = \cos 30° 41'$$

The trigonometric functions

If we are using only angles between 0° and 90°, then not only does 'sine' associate every angle with one and only one number, but every number (between 0 and 1) is associated with one and only one angle. Thus 'sine' can be described as a function which also has an inverse. This inverse function is usually written sin⁻¹, though ınv sin and arc

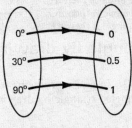

Fig. 17.10

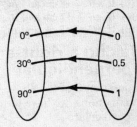

Fig. 17.11

sin are often shown at present on many calculators. If the domain is the set of angles between 0° and 90°, the range is the set of numbers from 0 to 1. Similarly with cosine and with tangent, though ın the latter case the range is the whole set of non-negative numbers.

Exercise 17a

1 Check your use of calculator or tables by finding

    (a) sin 21.4°   (b) cos 31.4°   (c) tan 41.4°
    (d) sin 51° 40'   (e) cos 61° 40'   (f) tan 71° 40'.

2 'The angle whose sine is . . .' is often abbreviated sin⁻¹ or arc sin or inv sin. Find

(a) the angle whose sine is 0.1

(b) $\sin^{-1}(0.2)$ (c) $\sin^{-1}(\frac{1}{3})$

(d) the angle whose cosine is 0.4

(e) $\cos^{-1}(0.5)$ (f) $\cos^{-1}(\frac{2}{3})$

(g) the angle whose tangent is 0.7

(h) $\tan^{-1}(0.8)$ (i) $\tan^{-1}(\frac{4}{3})$

3

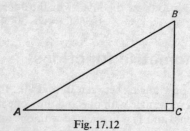

Fig. 17.12

Use Fig. 17.12.

(a) If $AB =$ 8 cm and $A = 41°$, find AC and BC.

(b) If $AB =$ 8 cm and $BC =$ 6.5 cm, find angle A then AC.

(c) If $AB = 12$ cm and $AC = 10$ cm, find angle A then BC.

(d) If $AC =$ 8 cm and $BC =$ 7 cm, find angle A then AB.

Making a right-angled triangle by drawing a perpendicular

In question **3** of the above, angle $C = 90°$. In many problems set in examinations, we have to make a right-angled triangle by drawing a perpendicular.

Example 17.2   *In Fig.* 17.13, *angle BAD = angle ADC = 90°, angle ACB = 66° and angle ACD = 41°. The length of AC = 7.5 cm. Calculate the lengths of AD and AB.*

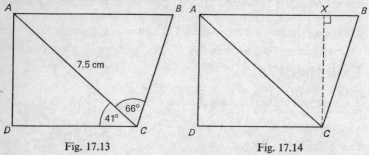

Fig. 17.13   Fig. 17.14

We can find the length of AD easily, as triangle ADC contains a right angle at D. Thus

$$\sin 41° = \frac{AD}{7.5},$$
$$\therefore AD = 7.5 \sin 41°$$
$$= 4.920, \text{ to three decimal places.}$$

Since there is not a right angle in triangle ABC, the easiest way to find the length of AB is to draw the line through C perpendicular to AB to meet AB in X.

Then $AX = CD = 7.5 \cos 41° = 5.660$
and $BX = CX \tan 17° = 1.504$
              $AB = 5.660 + 1.504 = 7.164.$

Alternatively, a line AY can be drawn through A perpendicular to BC and the right-angled triangles ACY, ABY used (*see* p. 160).

Example 17.3 *A man walks 50 m on a bearing of 050°, then 40 m on a bearing of 120°. Calculate the distance from his starting point O, and the bearing of his final position from his starting point.*

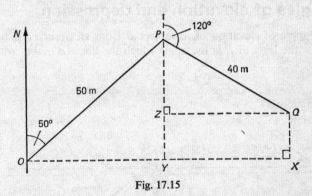

Fig. 17.15

Draw perpendiculars as in Fig. 17.15. The distance Q is east of O is $OY + YX$. To find OY, in triangle OPY, angle $OPY = 50°$ so that $\sin 50° = \frac{OY}{50}$, and $OY = 50 \sin 50° = 38.3$. In triangle PQZ, angle $QPZ = 60°$ so that $\sin 60° = \frac{ZQ}{40}$ and $ZQ = 40 \sin 60° = 34.64$. Thus his distance east of O is $(34.64 + 38.3)$ m, i.e. 72.94 m. His distance north of O is QX, and $QX = PY - PZ$. Now

$\cos 50° = \dfrac{PY}{50}$, so $PY = 50 \cos 50° = 32.14$ and similarly $PZ = 40 \cos 60° = 20$. So his distance north of O is $(32.14 - 20)$, i.e. 12.14 m. Applying Pythagoras' theorem to triangle OQX, (Fig. 17.16), we have

$$OQ^2 = (72.94)^2 + (12.14)^2$$
$$\simeq 5467$$
$$OQ \simeq 74,$$

the distance of Q from O is 74 m. To find the bearing of Q from O, $\tan QOX = \dfrac{12.14}{72.94}$, so angle $QOX \simeq 9°$, and the bearing of Q from O is 081°.

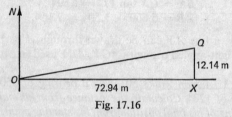

Fig. 17.16

Angles of elevation and depression

The angle of elevation of an object B from an observer A who is below the level of B is the angle which the line AB makes with the

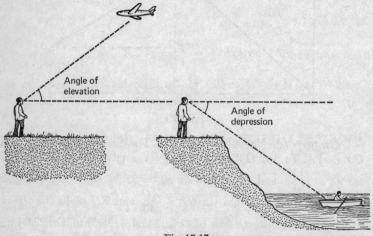

Fig. 17.17

horizontal. If C is below A, the angle of depression of C from A is the angle which AC makes with the horizontal.

N.B. Notice that both angles are measured with the horizontal and that the angle of elevation of B from A is equal to the angle of depression of A from B.

Example 17.4 *A man M on the top of a cliff 60 m high sees two buoys A and B whose angles of depression are 15.2° and 12.5°. The line AB is perpendicular to the plane of the cliff. What is the distance between the two buoys?*

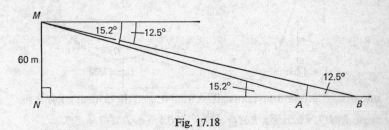

Fig. 17.18

Let MN represent the plane face of the cliff. Then $\tan 15.2° = \dfrac{60}{AN}$,

$$\text{so } AN = \frac{60}{\tan 15.2°} = 221,$$

and $\tan 12.5° = \dfrac{60}{BN}$,

$$\text{so } BN = \frac{60}{\tan 12.5°} = 271.$$

Thus $AB = 271 - 221 = 50$, the distance between the buoys is 50 metres.

Shortest distance to a straight line

The shortest distance from a point P to a given straight line l is the perpendicular from P on to l. This can be applied to many trigonometrical problems. If a boat starts from a mooring M 5 km due North of a rock R, and sails on a bearing of 160°, its shortest distance from the rock will be 5 sin 20° km, i.e. about 1.71 km. If for safety reasons the boat must not come within 0.5 km of the rock, the region

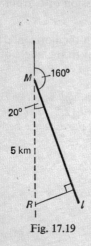

Fig. 17.19

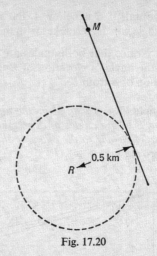

Fig. 17.20

into which the boat must not sail is circular, and the critical angle is the angle RMQ, where $\sin RMQ = \dfrac{0.5}{5} = 0.1$, i.e. $R\widehat{M}Q = 5.7°$.

Exercise 17b

1 In triangle ABC, $BC = 9.4$ cm, angle $BAC = 40°$ and angle $BCA = 30°$. Draw the line through B perpendicular to AC to meet AC at X. Calculate (a) BX (b) AB (c) CX (d) CA.

2 A man whose eyes are 1.8 m above the ground is 60 m from a vertical flagpole, height 20 m. Find (a) the angle of elevation of the top of the flagpole from the man's eyes; (b) the angle of elevation from the man's eyes of a knot halfway up the flag-pole.

3 A point T is 10 km due north of a point R. A point S is 8 km from T, and the bearing of S from T is 130°. Find the distance of S from R and the bearing of S from R.

4 Points A, B, and C lie in a straight line, such that $AB = 220$ m and $BC = 170$ m. A vertical tower BT at B is such that the angle of elevation of the top of the tower T from A is 10°. Find the angle of elevation of T from C.

5 An observer O is placed on a straight road running east–west. A gun G is 4 km from O, on a bearing of 070°. If shells from the gun can just reach the road, calculate the range of the gun. If, however, the range is 2 km, find the length of roadway within range of the gun.

18 Sine and cosine formulae, three-dimensional problems

Sine formula

Using Fig. 18.1, in which AD is perpendicular to BC, from triangle ABD, $AD = AB \sin B$ and from triangle ACD $AD = AC \sin C$, so that $\dfrac{b}{\sin B} = \dfrac{c}{\sin C}$. Similarly, drawing a line through B perpendicular to AC, $\dfrac{a}{\sin A} = \dfrac{c}{\sin C}$, whence

$$\frac{a}{\sin A} = \frac{b}{\sin B} = \frac{c}{\sin C}$$

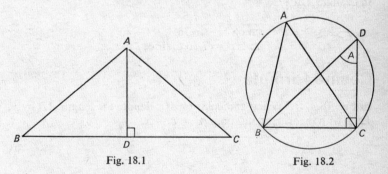

Fig. 18.1　　　　　　　　　Fig. 18.2

For an alternative proof, draw the circumcircle of triangle ABC and then the diameter through B. From triangle BCD, angle BDC = angle A (angles in same segment) and angle $BCD = 90°$ (angle in a semi-circle), so that $BC = BD \sin BDC$.

i.e. $2R = \dfrac{a}{\sin A}$, where R is the radius of the circumcircle. Similarly,

$2R = \dfrac{b}{\sin B}$ and $2R = \dfrac{c}{\sin C}$ so that

$$\frac{a}{\sin A} = \frac{b}{\sin B} = \frac{c}{\sin C} = 2R.$$

The symmetry of this result should be noticed.

Example 18.1 *Using the data on page 154, find AB using the sine formula.*

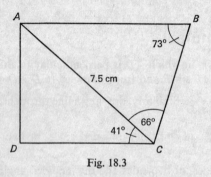

Fig. 18.3

In triangle ABC,

$$\frac{AB}{\sin 66^\circ} = \frac{7.5}{\sin 73^\circ}$$
$$\therefore \ AB = 7.16, \text{to three s.f.}$$

Cosine formula

In Fig. 18.4, BD is perpendicular to AC; denote the length AD by x. Then with the usual notation, $DC = b - x$.

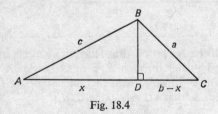

Fig. 18.4

From triangle ABD,

$$BD^2 = c^2 - x^2$$

and from triangle BCD,

$$BD^2 = a^2 - (b - x)^2$$

whence

$$c^2 - x^2 = a^2 - (b - x)^2$$

so that

$$c^2 = a^2 - b^2 + 2bx$$

but

$$x = c \cos A,$$

so

$$a^2 = b^2 + c^2 - 2bc \cos A.$$

This formula enables us to find the third side of a triangle, knowing two sides and the included angle. To find one angle of a triangle, change the subject of the equation so that

$$\cos A = \frac{b^2 + c^2 - a^2}{2bc}.$$

To solve triangles that do not have a right angle

Given two sides and one not-included angle, or two angles and one side, **use the sine formula.**

Given three sides, or two sides and the included angle, **use the cosine formula.**

Example 18.2 *In triangle PQR, $PQ = 7$ cm, $PR = 8$ cm, and angle $PQR = 50°$. Calculate the angle PRQ.*

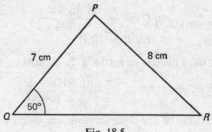

Fig. 18.5

Using the sine formula,

$$\frac{7}{\sin PRQ} = \frac{8}{\sin 50°}$$

$$\sin PRQ = \frac{7 \sin 50°}{8}$$

$$\therefore \text{ angle } PRQ = 42°$$

Example 18.3 *In triangle PQR, PQ = 7 cm, QR = 8 cm and angle PQR = 50°. Find the length of PR and the angle QPR.*

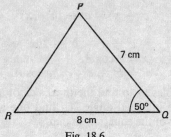

Fig. 18.6

$$PR^2 = PQ^2 + QR^2 - 2 \times PQ \times QR \cos 50°$$
$$= 7^2 + 8^2 - 2 \times 7 \times 8 \cos 50°$$
$$= 49 + 64 - 71.99$$
$$= 41.01$$
$$PR = 6.404, \text{ to 4 s.f.}$$

N.B. Take care to find first the product $2 \times 7 \times 8 \cos 50°$, then subtract it from $7^2 + 8^2$; it is only too easy to make the mistake of calculating $(7^2 + 8^2 - 2 \times 7 \times 8) \cos 50°$.

To find angle *QPR*, use the sine formula.

$$\frac{\sin QPR}{8} = \frac{\sin 50°}{6.404}$$
$$\sin QPR = \frac{8 \sin 50°}{6.404}$$
$$\therefore \widehat{QPR} = 73.1°$$

We could have used the cosine formula, in the form

$$\cos QPR = \frac{7^2 + (6.404)^2 - 8^2}{2 \times 7 \times 6.404}$$

but the calculations of the sine formula are usually easier to carry out, whether using calculator or not.

Note on the use of calculators

Always set out clearly, as above, the calculations being performed on the calculator. This enables us to see exactly what calculations we are carrying out, and enables an examiner to follow our working

It is, of course, always important to carry out a rough check of our calculations, and to beware of ambiguity in the use of the $\sin^{-1}$ function (*see* question 2).

Exercise 18a

1 In triangle ABC, $AB = 8.4$ cm, angle $B = 44°$, and angle $C = 64°$. Find angle A and the lengths of the other two sides.
2 In triangle ABC, $AB = 8.4$ cm, $BC = 7.4$ cm, and angle $A = 40°$. Use the sine formula to find angle ACB, given that this angle is acute, and then find angle ABC and the length of AC.
   Make a scale drawing to show that there are two possible triangles that can be drawn from the data, and that in one of them angle ACB is obtuse. Calculate angle ABC and the length of AC in this case.
3 In triangle ABC, $AB = 8$ cm, $BC = 7$ cm, and $AC = 5$ cm. Calculate the angles of the triangle.
4 In triangle ABC, $AB = 8.4$ cm, $BC = 7.8$ cm, and angle $ABC = 80°$. Calculate the length of AC and the angles A and C in the triangle.

Latitude and longtitude

In Fig. 18.7 N and S represent the North and South poles. The line SN is the axis of the Earth. The circle BQA represents the Equator.

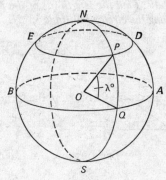

Fig. 18.7

A **great circle** is a section of the Earth's surface by any plane through the centre O. The **shortest distance** between two points on the surface of the earth is the minor arc of the great circle through those two points.

A **meridian of longitude** is a great circle (here NPQS) which passes through the north and south poles; a **parallel of latitude** is a section of the Earth's surface by a plane parallel to the Equator (here *DPE*).

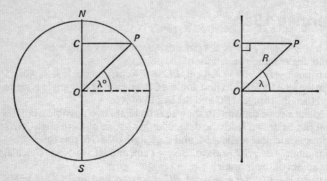

Fig. 18.8

Looking at the section of the earth in Fig. 18.8, we see that the radius of a circle of latitude angle λ is $R \cos \lambda$, where R is the radius of the earth.

Example 18.4 *An aeroplane is to fly from a point P 35° N 30° E to a point Q 35° N 150° W. Find the length (a) of the path over the North Pole, (b) the path along the circle of latitude 35° N.*

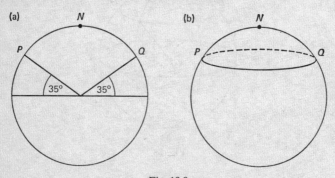

Fig. 18.9

The path over the North Pole is part of a great circle (Fig. 18.9a) Since it subtends an angle 110° at the centre, the length of the path is

$\frac{110}{360} \times 2\pi R$, where R is the radius of the Earth. Taking R to be 6400 km, the length of the path over the North Pole is 12 300 km, to 3 s.f.

The path around the circle of latitude 35° N is exactly half the circumference of that circle (from 30° E to 150° W is 180°), so the length of the path around the circle latitude is $\frac{1}{2} \times 2\pi R \cos 35°$ i.e. 16 500 km, to 3 s.f.

Exercise 18b

(Take the radius of the Earth to be 6400 km.)

1 Two towns on the Equator differ in longitude by 34°. Find the distance between them, along the equator.

2 Two towns on latitude 40° S differ in longitude by 34°. Find the distance between them along the circle of latitude.

3 Two towns on latitude 20° S differ in longitude by 180°. Find the distance between them (a) over the South Pole, (b) around the circle of latitude 20° S.

Three-dimensional problems

A straight line perpendicular to a plane is perpendicular to every line in the plane. Thus an edge of a rectangular box is perpendicular

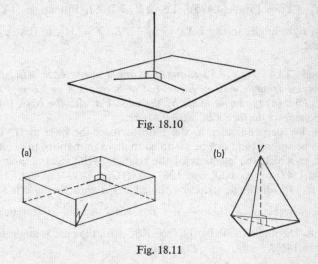

Fig. 18.10

(a)   (b)

Fig. 18.11

to every line in the face adjacent to that edge (Fig. 18.11a), and any line drawn through the vertex of a pyramid perpendicular to the base is perpendicular to every line in the base (Fig. 18.11b).

Example 18.5 *Fig. 18.12 shows a right prism whose cross-section is an isosceles triangle ABC. AB = BC = 12 cm; angle ABC = 44°. Find the angle made by AE with the horizontal plane ACFD.*

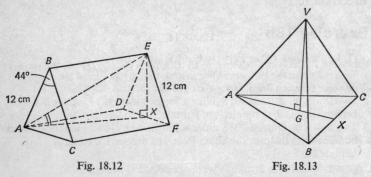

Fig. 18.12   Fig. 18.13

Draw the line EX perpendicular to the plane $ACFD$. Then triangle DEX has a right angle at X, so that $\sin 22° = \dfrac{DX}{12}$, so $DX = 12 \sin 22° = 4.495$; similarly $EX = 12 \cos 22° = 11.13$. From triangle ADX, $AX^2 = 16^2 + (4.495)^2$, i.e. $AX = 16.62$. But angle AXE is also a right angle, so $\tan EAX = \dfrac{11.12}{16.62}$, $EAX = 34°$, to the nearest degree.

Example 18.6 *Fig. 18.13 shows a pyramid whose base ABC is an equilateral triangle. AB = BC = CA = 6 cm; VA = VB = VC = 8 cm. Find (a) the angle made by the edge VA with the base, (b) the angle made by the face VBC with the base.*

Draw VG perpendicular to the base to meet the base at G. Then G can be shown (and can be assumed in an examination) to be at the point at which the medians of the triangle ABC meet. Using Fig. 18.14a, $AD = 6 \cos 30° = 5.196$, so $AG = \frac{2}{3}AD = 3.464$. From Fig. 18.14b, the angle made by the edge VA with the base is angle VAG, where $\cos VAG = \dfrac{3.464}{8}$, i.e. $VAG = 64°$, to the nearest degree. The angle made by the face VBC with the base is angle VDA (Fig. 18.14b).

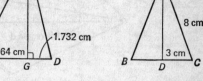

Fig. 18.14

Applying Pythagoras' theorem to triangle VBD, $DV = 7.416$, so $\cos VDA = \dfrac{1.732}{7.416}$, i.e. $VDA = 76°$, to the nearest degree.

Exercise 18c

1 A road sign is in the form of a vertical equilateral triangle ABC, with AC horizontal and length 1 m. When the angle of elevation of the sun is 40° and the rays are at right angles to AC, the shadow of B is at B', a point on the horizontal plane through AC. Find the distance of B' from AC.

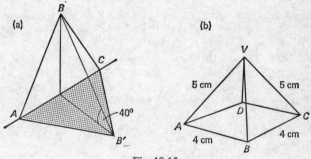

Fig. 18.15

2 Fig. 18.15b shows a pyramid vertex V on a square base $ABCD$. Each side of the square is 4 cm long, and the edges through V are each 5 cm long. Find by calculation the angle made by the edge VA with the base, and the angle made by the face VAB with the base.

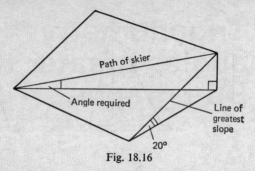

Fig. 18.16

3 Descending a hill of gradient 20°, a skier travels in a straight line
which makes an angle of 45° with the line of greatest slope. Find the
angle between his path and the horizontal. (*Hint:* suppose that he travels
100 m down his path. Find the distance travelled in the direction of the
line of greatest slope, and then the vertical distance he has descended.)

19 Trigonometry: angles greater than 90°, graphs

We have considered so far only the ratios of acute angles. If we wish to extend the domain over which we define the trig functions, then we have to redefine the functions, in a manner consistent with the earlier definition.

Projections

If OP is a line length of 1 unit, inclined to a base line (taken as Ox) at an angle θ, then the projection on the x-axis is equal to $\cos \theta$, and

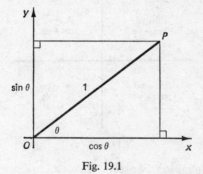

Fig. 19.1

the projection on to the y-axis is $\sin \theta$, using the existing definitions in the right-angled triangle shown. If, however, we *define* cosine as the projection of a line 1 unit long on the x-axis, then this definition can apply to all angles, positive or negative, and is also consistent with our earlier definition. We define sine as the projection of a line 1 unit long on the y-axis, and tangent as the ratio $\dfrac{\text{sine}}{\text{cosine}}$.

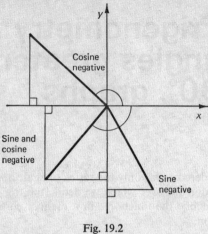

Fig. 19.2

Fig. 19.2 shows that the cosine and sine of certain angles can be negative, and Fig. 19.3 gives the signs of each of these depending on the quadrant in which the angle lies.

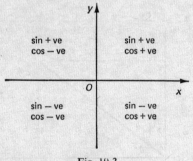

Fig. 19.3

Using these definitions, we see

$$\sin (180 - x)° = \quad \sin x°, \cos (180 - x)° = -\cos x°$$
$$\sin (180 + x)° = -\sin x°, \cos (180 + x)° = -\cos x°$$
$$\sin (360 - x)° = -\sin x°, \cos (360 - x)° = \quad \cos x°$$

and so on, for angles of any magnitude.

Exercise 19a

Use calculators (or tables) and rough sketches to find:

1 sin 120°; sin 150°; sin 200°; sin 240°; sin 310°.
2 cos 120°; cos 150°; cos 200°; cos 240°; cos 310°.
3 tan 120°; tan 150°; tan 200°; tan 240°; tan 310°.
4 sin (−30)°; cos (−30)°; tan (−30)°.

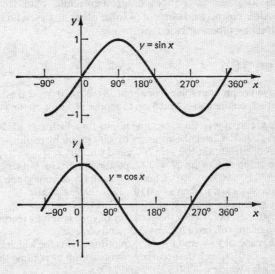

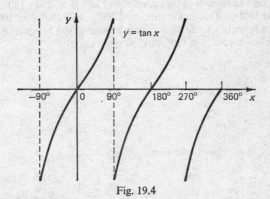

Fig. 19.4

Graph of y = sin x

Using some of the values found above, and any extra values needed, we can draw the graph of $y = \sin x$, for values of x from $-360°$ to $+360°$, (Fig. 19.4), also $y = \cos x$, and $y = \tan x$ over the same set of values. Study the graphs and draw them again, calculating the values of y at intervals of $30°$ or $60°$. Check that your graphs have no 'bumps' or sudden changes of gradient, and read from your graphs the sine, cosine, and tangent of some other angles, which should be checked using tables or calculator.

Exercise 19b

The scale given requires graph paper about 28 cm by 20 cm. Take 2 cm to represent $30°$ on the x-axis, and 5 cm to represent 1 unit on the y-axis.

1 Draw the graph of $y = \sin x$, plotting points for which $x = 0°, 30°,$ $60°, 90°, \ldots 360°$. Check the accuracy of your graph by reading the values of $\sin 80°$, $\sin 100°$, $\sin 260°$, and $\sin 280°$.

2 Draw the graph of $y = \sin (x - 30°)$, plotting points for which $x = 0°, 30°, 60°, 90° \ldots 360°$. Check the accuracy of your graph by reading the values of y when $x = 110°, 130°, 290°$, and $310°$.

3 Draw the graph of $y = \cos x$, plotting points for which $x = 0°,$ $30°, 60°, 90° \ldots 360°$. Check the accuracy of your graph by reading the values of $\cos 10°$, $\cos 170°$, $\cos 200°$, and $\cos 340°$.

4 Draw the graph of $y = \cos (x - 40°)$, plotting points for which $x = 0°,$ $30°, 60° \ldots 360°$. Check the accuracy of your graph by reading the values of y for which $x = 50°, 210°$, and $240°$.

5 Draw the graph of $y = \tan x$, plotting points for which $x = 0°, 30°,$ $45°, 60°$, on one branch of the curve, then $120°, 135°, 150°, 180°, 210°,$ $225°$, and $240°$ on a second branch, and $300°, 315°, 330°$, and $360°$ on a third branch. Check the accuracy of your graph by reading the values of $\tan 50°$, $\tan 130°$, $\tan 230°$, and $\tan 310°$.

20 Matrices

Notes on matrices

Two matrices can only be added together if they have the same number of rows and columns, e.g.

$$\begin{pmatrix} a & b \\ c & d \end{pmatrix} + \begin{pmatrix} x & y \\ z & w \end{pmatrix} = \begin{pmatrix} a+x & b+y \\ c+z & d+w \end{pmatrix}$$

but $\begin{pmatrix} a & b \\ c & d \end{pmatrix}$ and $\begin{pmatrix} x \\ z \end{pmatrix}$ cannot be added together.

The matrix **A** can only multiply the matrix **B** if **A** has the same number of columns as **B** has rows,

e.g. $\begin{pmatrix} a & b \\ c & d \end{pmatrix}\begin{pmatrix} x \\ z \end{pmatrix}$ exists but $\begin{pmatrix} x \\ z \end{pmatrix}\begin{pmatrix} a & b \\ c & d \end{pmatrix}$ does not.

To multiply two matrices, each row of the first 'dives down' the corresponding row of the second,

$$\begin{pmatrix} a & b \\ c & d \end{pmatrix}\begin{pmatrix} x \\ z \end{pmatrix} = \begin{pmatrix} ax+bz \\ cx+dz \end{pmatrix}$$

N.B. Matrix multiplication is not commutative; in general, **A . B** $\neq$ **B . A**.

The inverse of the 2×2 matrix $\begin{pmatrix} a & b \\ c & d \end{pmatrix}$

is $$\frac{1}{ad-bc}\begin{pmatrix} d & -b \\ -c & a \end{pmatrix}.$$

Definition

Matrices are arrays of numbers, which may have been set out so that they display information conveniently, and which are subject to certain laws of combination, especially addition and multiplication.

Examples of matrices displaying information

Letters posted by a small company one week:

	First Class	Second Class
Monday	12	25
Tuesday	24	35
Wednesday	28	40
Thursday	16	30
Friday	36	40

(1)

The route matrix below describes the routes in Fig. 20.1, where there is a road from town A to town X, but no road from town B to town X.

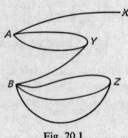

Fig. 20.1

$$\begin{array}{cc} & \begin{array}{ccc} X & Y & Z \end{array} \\ \begin{array}{c} A \\ B \end{array} & \begin{pmatrix} 1 & 2 & 0 \\ 0 & 1 & 3 \end{pmatrix} \end{array}$$

(2)

Matrix addition

Add the corresponding elements, thus

$$\begin{pmatrix} 2 & 1 & 3 \\ 1 & 0 & 4 \end{pmatrix} + \begin{pmatrix} 3 & -1 & -2 \\ 4 & 0 & -2 \end{pmatrix} = \begin{pmatrix} 5 & 0 & 1 \\ 5 & 0 & 2 \end{pmatrix}$$

Since we have to add corresponding elements, matrices must have the same number of rows and columns if they are to be added (or subtracted), thus

$$\begin{pmatrix} 4 & 1 \\ 1 & 2 \end{pmatrix} \text{ cannot be added to } \begin{pmatrix} 5 \\ 2 \end{pmatrix}.$$

Scalar multiples

Twice a matrix **A** is written 2**A**, where we double each element in matrix **A**, e.g.

if $\qquad \mathbf{A} = \begin{pmatrix} 2 & 0 & -1 \\ \frac{1}{2} & 0 & 4 \end{pmatrix}, 2\mathbf{A} = \begin{pmatrix} 4 & 0 & -2 \\ 1 & 0 & 8 \end{pmatrix}$

Example 20.1 *If* $\quad \mathbf{A} = \begin{pmatrix} 2 & 1 \\ 4 & -1 \end{pmatrix}, \mathbf{B} = \begin{pmatrix} 1 & 0 \\ 1 & 2 \end{pmatrix},$ *and*
$\mathbf{C} = \begin{pmatrix} 4 & 5 & 6 \\ 3 & 2 & 1 \end{pmatrix},$ *find, if possible*

(*a*) **A** + **B**, (*b*) **A** + **C**, (*c*) 3**A**, (*d*) $\frac{1}{2}$**C**.

Since **A** and **B** both have two rows and two columns (and so are called '2 by 2 matrices'), we can find their sum.

$$\mathbf{A} + \mathbf{B} = \begin{pmatrix} 3 & 1 \\ 5 & 1 \end{pmatrix}$$

Since **A** has two columns and **C** has three columns, we cannot add them together, so that **A** + **C** does not exist.

$$3\mathbf{A} = 3\begin{pmatrix} 2 & 1 \\ 4 & -1 \end{pmatrix} = \begin{pmatrix} 6 & 3 \\ 12 & -3 \end{pmatrix}$$

and $\qquad \frac{1}{2}\mathbf{C} = \frac{1}{2}\begin{pmatrix} 4 & 5 & 6 \\ 3 & 2 & 1 \end{pmatrix} = \begin{pmatrix} 2 & \frac{5}{2} & 3 \\ \frac{3}{2} & 1 & \frac{1}{2} \end{pmatrix}$

Multiplication of matrices

If $\qquad \mathbf{A} = \begin{pmatrix} 1 & 2 \\ 3 & 4 \end{pmatrix}$ and $\mathbf{B} = \begin{pmatrix} 5 & 6 & 7 \\ 8 & 9 & 0 \end{pmatrix}$

to find the product **A** . **B** we let each row of **A** 'dive down' the corresponding column of **B**, multiplying the associated elements and adding these products, thus

$$\mathbf{A} \cdot \mathbf{B} = \begin{pmatrix} \boxed{1 \ 2} \\ 3 \ 4 \end{pmatrix}\begin{pmatrix} 5 & 6 & 7 \\ 8 & 9 & 0 \end{pmatrix} = \begin{pmatrix} 5\boxed{1} & 6 & 7 \\ 8\boxed{2} & 9 & 0 \end{pmatrix}$$

to find the element in the first row and first column of **A . B**. This element is $1 \times 5 + 2 \times 8$, i.e. 21. To find the element in the first row and third column of **A . B**, let the first row of **A** 'dive down' the third column of **B**,

$$\begin{pmatrix} 5 & 6 & 7 \boxed{1} \\ 8 & 9 & 0 \boxed{2} \end{pmatrix}$$

so the element in the first row, third column is $1 \times 7 + 2 \times 0$, i.e. 7. So far we have found that

$$\mathbf{A} . \mathbf{B} = \begin{pmatrix} 21 & - & 7 \\ - & - & - \end{pmatrix}$$

The missing entries are found in the same way, so that

$$\mathbf{A} . \mathbf{B} = \begin{pmatrix} 21 & 24 & 7 \\ 47 & 54 & 21 \end{pmatrix}$$

Since **B** has 3 columns and **A** has only two rows we cannot find the product **B . A.**, for

$$\mathbf{B} . \mathbf{A} = \begin{pmatrix} \boxed{5 \quad 6 \quad 7} \\ 8 \quad 9 \quad 0 \end{pmatrix} \begin{pmatrix} 1 & 2 \\ 3 & 4 \end{pmatrix} = \begin{pmatrix} 1\boxed{5} & 2 \\ 3\boxed{6} & 4 \\ ?\boxed{7} & \end{pmatrix}$$

N.B. Matrix multiplication is not commutative, in general **A . B** $\neq$ **B . A**.

Zero matrix, identity matrix

A matrix with every element zero is called a zero matrix, e.g. $\begin{pmatrix} 0 & 0 \\ 0 & 0 \end{pmatrix}$ is the zero matrix of order two; a matrix with a 1 in every element of the leading diagonal and a zero everywhere else is called a unit matrix, e.g. $\begin{pmatrix} 1 & 0 \\ 0 & 1 \end{pmatrix}$ is the unit matrix of order two.

Equal matrices

Two matrices are equal if and only if every element of one is equal to the corresponding element of the other, thus if

$$\begin{pmatrix} a & b \\ c & d \end{pmatrix} = \begin{pmatrix} 3 & 4 \\ 5 & 6 \end{pmatrix}, a = 3, b = 4, c = 5, d = 6$$

This often enables us to solve certain equations.

Example 20.2

If $$\begin{pmatrix} a & 3a \\ 2b & b \end{pmatrix}\begin{pmatrix} 2 \\ 3 \end{pmatrix} = \begin{pmatrix} 44 \\ 42 \end{pmatrix} \text{ find } a \text{ and } b.$$

Multiplying, $$\begin{pmatrix} a & 3a \\ 2b & b \end{pmatrix}\begin{pmatrix} 2 \\ 3 \end{pmatrix} = \begin{pmatrix} 11a \\ 7b \end{pmatrix}$$

$$\therefore \qquad \begin{pmatrix} 11a \\ 7b \end{pmatrix} = \begin{pmatrix} 44 \\ 42 \end{pmatrix},$$

$11a = 44, 7b = 42$; so that $a = 4$ and $b = 6$.

Exercise 20a

1 If $\mathbf{A} = \begin{pmatrix} 2 & -1 \\ 4 & 3 \end{pmatrix}$, $\mathbf{B} = \begin{pmatrix} 3 & 0 \\ 5 & 1 \end{pmatrix}$, $\mathbf{C} = \begin{pmatrix} 2 \\ 3 \end{pmatrix}$, $\mathbf{D} = (2 \quad -1)$,

   find (a) $\mathbf{A} + \mathbf{B}$ (b) $\mathbf{A} - 2\mathbf{B}$ (c) $3\mathbf{A} + 2\mathbf{B}$ (d) $\mathbf{A} \cdot \mathbf{B}$

       (e) $\mathbf{B} \cdot \mathbf{A}$ (f) $\mathbf{A} \cdot \mathbf{C}$ (g) $\mathbf{B} \cdot \mathbf{C}$ (h) $\mathbf{D} \cdot \mathbf{A}$

       (i) $\mathbf{D} \cdot \mathbf{B}$ (j) $\mathbf{C} \cdot \mathbf{D}$ (к) $\mathbf{D} \cdot \mathbf{C}$ (l) $\mathbf{A}^2$

   What happens when we try to find $\mathbf{A} \cdot \mathbf{D}$?

2 If $\begin{pmatrix} 1 & -3 \\ 4 & x \end{pmatrix}\begin{pmatrix} y \\ 5 \end{pmatrix} = \begin{pmatrix} 1 \\ 4 \end{pmatrix}$ find the values of x and y.

3 If $\begin{pmatrix} 0 & 4 \\ 3 & -1 \end{pmatrix}\begin{pmatrix} a \\ b \end{pmatrix} = \begin{pmatrix} -12 \\ a \end{pmatrix}$ find the values of a and b.

4 Multiply each side of the matrix equation

$$\begin{pmatrix} 5 & 2 \\ 3 & 1 \end{pmatrix}\begin{pmatrix} x \\ y \end{pmatrix} = \begin{pmatrix} 4 \\ 4 \end{pmatrix}$$

by the matrix $\begin{pmatrix} 1 & -2 \\ -3 & 5 \end{pmatrix}$ and so find x and y.

5 If $\mathbf{A} = \begin{pmatrix} 0 & -1 \\ 1 & 0 \end{pmatrix}$, find $\mathbf{A}^2$ and $\mathbf{A}^3$, and show that $\mathbf{A}^4$ is the two by two unit matrix.

6 Let $\mathbf{A}$ be the matrix (1) on page 174. If it costs 9p to send a letter first class and 7p to send a letter second class, let $\mathbf{B} = \begin{pmatrix} 9 \\ 7 \end{pmatrix}$. Form the matrix product $\mathbf{A} \cdot \mathbf{B}$, and interpret your answer. Let $\mathbf{C} = (1 \quad 1 \quad 1 \quad 1 \quad 1)$. Form the matrix products $\mathbf{C} \cdot \mathbf{A}$, $\mathbf{C} \cdot (\mathbf{A} \cdot \mathbf{B})$, and interpret each answer.

7

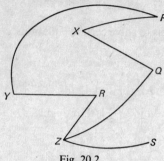

Fig. 20.2

Let **A** be matrix (2) on page 174. Let **B** be the route matrix that describes the routes between X, Y, and Z and P, Q, R, and S. Write down the matrix **B** and find the product **A . B**. What is the interpretation of the element in the first row and third column?

8 In 1880, England beat Wales at Rugby Football, scoring 7 goals, 1 dropped goal, and 6 tries, while Wales failed to score. Display this information in a matrix **A** with two rows and three columns.

Taking the later scoring values of 5 points for a goal, 4 for a dropped goal, and 3 for a try, form a matrix **B** such that the product **A . B** gives the scores of each team in this match. Form another matrix **C** giving the scores of 6 points for a goal, 4 for a try, and 3 for a dropped goal, so that the product **A . C** gives the scores for this match.

Determinant of a matrix

The determinant of the 2×2 matrix $\begin{pmatrix} a & b \\ c & d \end{pmatrix}$ is $ad - bc$, e.g. the determinant of $\begin{pmatrix} 3 & 1 \\ 2 & 5 \end{pmatrix}$ is $3 \times 5 - 2 \times 1$, i.e. 13 and of $\begin{pmatrix} 3 & -1 \\ 2 & 4 \end{pmatrix}$ is $3 \times 4 - 2 \times (-1)$, i.e. 14.

A matrix whose determinant is zero e.g. $\begin{pmatrix} 2 & 4 \\ 1 & 2 \end{pmatrix}$ is called a **singular** matrix.

Inverse matrix

The inverse of a matrix **A** (written $\mathbf{A}^{-1}$) is the matrix such that $\mathbf{A} \cdot \mathbf{A}^{-1} = \mathbf{A}^{-1} \cdot \mathbf{A} = \mathbf{I}$, where $\mathbf{I}$ is the appropriate unit matrix.

Thus $\begin{pmatrix} 5 & 3 \\ -2 & -1 \end{pmatrix} \begin{pmatrix} -1 & -3 \\ 2 & 5 \end{pmatrix} = \begin{pmatrix} -1 & -3 \\ 2 & 5 \end{pmatrix} \begin{pmatrix} 5 & 3 \\ -2 & -1 \end{pmatrix} = \begin{pmatrix} 1 & 0 \\ 0 & 1 \end{pmatrix}$

so that $\begin{pmatrix} -1 & -3 \\ 2 & 5 \end{pmatrix}$ is the inverse of $\begin{pmatrix} 5 & 3 \\ -2 & -1 \end{pmatrix}$

and also $\begin{pmatrix} 5 & 3 \\ -2 & -1 \end{pmatrix}$ is the inverse of $\begin{pmatrix} -1 & -3 \\ 2 & 5 \end{pmatrix}$

In general, to find the inverse of the matrix $\begin{pmatrix} a & b \\ c & d \end{pmatrix}$ interchange the two elements in the leading diagonal $\begin{pmatrix} d & \\ & a \end{pmatrix}$, and change the sign of the other two $\begin{pmatrix} d & -b \\ -c & a \end{pmatrix}$, then divide by the value of the determinant $(ad - bc)$, so the inverse is $\dfrac{1}{ad-bc}\begin{pmatrix} d & -b \\ -c & a \end{pmatrix}$.

N.B. In the matrix $\begin{pmatrix} 5 & 3 \\ -2 & -1 \end{pmatrix}$ the determinant is 1 so that we have only to interchange 5 and -1 then change the signs of the other elements.

Example 20.3 *Find the inverse of* $\begin{pmatrix} 6 & 3 \\ 3 & 4 \end{pmatrix}$.

Interchange the elements in the leading diagonal: $\begin{pmatrix} 4 & \\ & 6 \end{pmatrix}$, change the signs of the other two: $\begin{pmatrix} 4 & -3 \\ -3 & 6 \end{pmatrix}$, divide by the value of the determinant, $6\times4 - 3\times3$, i.e. 15, so the inverse is $\dfrac{1}{15}\begin{pmatrix} 4 & -3 \\ -3 & 6 \end{pmatrix}$.

Exercise 20b

1 Find the value of the determinant of each of the following matrices:

(a) $\begin{pmatrix} 2 & 5 \\ 1 & 4 \end{pmatrix}$ (b) $\begin{pmatrix} 2 & 5 \\ -1 & 4 \end{pmatrix}$ (c) $\begin{pmatrix} 3 & 4 \\ 2 & 3 \end{pmatrix}$ (d) $\begin{pmatrix} 3 & 1 \\ 1 & 0 \end{pmatrix}$

2 Which of the following matrices is singular?

(a) $\begin{pmatrix} 2 & 4 \\ \frac{1}{2} & 1 \end{pmatrix}$ (b) $\begin{pmatrix} 2 & 1 \\ 0 & 0 \end{pmatrix}$ (c) $\begin{pmatrix} 0 & 1 \\ 1 & 0 \end{pmatrix}$ (d) $\begin{pmatrix} 1 & 1 \\ -1 & 1 \end{pmatrix}$

3 Find the inverse of each of the following matrices:

(a) $\begin{pmatrix} 2 & 1 \\ 4 & 3 \end{pmatrix}$ (b) $\begin{pmatrix} 3 & 1 \\ 5 & 2 \end{pmatrix}$ (c) $\begin{pmatrix} 3 & -1 \\ 5 & 2 \end{pmatrix}$

(d) $\begin{pmatrix} 2 & 4 \\ -\frac{1}{2} & 2 \end{pmatrix}$ (e) $\begin{pmatrix} 2 & 0 \\ 0 & 2 \end{pmatrix}$ (f) $\begin{pmatrix} 2 & 1 \\ 1 & 0 \end{pmatrix}$

4 If $M = \begin{pmatrix} 3 & 2 \\ -1 & 2 \end{pmatrix}$, find M^{-1}. Hence find x and y, if

$M \begin{pmatrix} x \\ y \end{pmatrix} = \begin{pmatrix} 13 \\ 1 \end{pmatrix}$.

5 If $M = \begin{pmatrix} 3 & -2 \\ 1 & 1 \end{pmatrix}$, find x and y when $M\begin{pmatrix} x \\ y \end{pmatrix} = \begin{pmatrix} 1 \\ 1 \end{pmatrix}$.

6 If $M = \begin{pmatrix} 4 & 2 \\ 1 & 3 \end{pmatrix}$, $x = \begin{pmatrix} x \\ y \end{pmatrix}$ and $M.x = p$,

find x and y when $p =$

(a) $\begin{pmatrix} 10 \\ -1 \end{pmatrix}$ (b) $\begin{pmatrix} 2 \\ 4 \end{pmatrix}$ (c) $\begin{pmatrix} 1 \\ 0 \end{pmatrix}$.

7 The simultaneous equations $3x + 4y = 2$, $x + 2y = 0$ may be written in matrix form $\begin{pmatrix} 3 & 4 \\ 1 & 2 \end{pmatrix}\begin{pmatrix} x \\ y \end{pmatrix} = \begin{pmatrix} 2 \\ 0 \end{pmatrix}$.

Find the inverse of the matrix $\begin{pmatrix} 3 & 4 \\ 1 & 2 \end{pmatrix}$ and hence solve the simultaneous equations for x and y.

8 Use a matrix method to solve the following pairs of simultaneous equations:

(a) $2x + 3y = 1$, $x + 5y = -3$
(b) $2x + 3y = -2$, $x + 5y = -3$
(c) $2x + 3y = 1$, $x + 5y = 1$

21 Geometrical applications of matrices

Mappings

Since matrices can be used to display information, a matrix can give the coordinates of a point, $\begin{pmatrix} x \\ y \end{pmatrix}$ or some times $(x \quad y)$, in two dimensions, or all the vertices of a polygon, e.g.

$$\begin{pmatrix} 0 & 1 & 1 & 0 \\ 0 & 0 & 1 & 1 \end{pmatrix}$$

represents the unit square (Fig. 21.1).

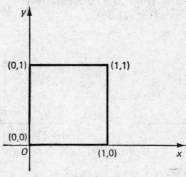

Fig. 21.1

Multiplication by a matrix maps the unit square into another figure, e.g. since

$$\begin{pmatrix} 3 & 2 \\ -1 & 1 \end{pmatrix}\begin{pmatrix} 0 & 1 & 1 & 0 \\ 0 & 0 & 1 & 1 \end{pmatrix} = \begin{pmatrix} 0 & 3 & 5 & 2 \\ 0 & -1 & 0 & 1 \end{pmatrix}$$

the matrix $\begin{pmatrix} 3 & 2 \\ -1 & 1 \end{pmatrix}$ transforms the unit square into the parallelogram $OPQR$ (Fig. 21.2). It is often easy to describe by a matrix a transformation that would be almost impossible to describe by words.

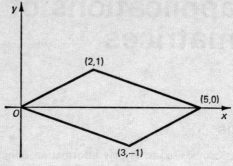

Fig. 21.2

Reflection

Since $\begin{pmatrix} 1 & 0 \\ 0 & -1 \end{pmatrix}\begin{pmatrix} x \\ y \end{pmatrix} = \begin{pmatrix} x \\ -y \end{pmatrix}$, the matrix $\begin{pmatrix} 1 & 0 \\ 0 & -1 \end{pmatrix}$ describes a reflection in the x-axis (Fig. 21.3a). Similarly $\begin{pmatrix} -1 & 0 \\ 0 & 1 \end{pmatrix}$ describes a reflection in the y-axis (Fig. 21.3b).

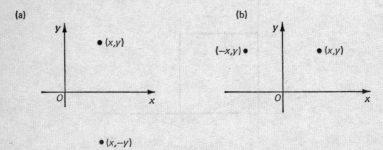

Fig. 21.3

Since $\begin{pmatrix} 0 & 1 \\ 1 & 0 \end{pmatrix}\begin{pmatrix} x \\ y \end{pmatrix} = \begin{pmatrix} y \\ x \end{pmatrix}$ the matrix $\begin{pmatrix} 0 & 1 \\ 1 & 0 \end{pmatrix}$ describes a reflection in the line $y = x$, and similarly $\begin{pmatrix} 0 & -1 \\ -1 & 0 \end{pmatrix}$ describes reflection in the line $y = -x$ (Fig. 21.4a and b).

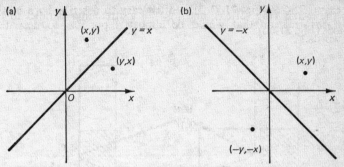

Fig. 21.4

Rotation

Since $\begin{pmatrix} 0 & 1 \\ -1 & 0 \end{pmatrix}\begin{pmatrix} x \\ y \end{pmatrix} = \begin{pmatrix} y \\ -x \end{pmatrix}$, the matrix $\mathbf{R} = \begin{pmatrix} 0 & 1 \\ -1 & 0 \end{pmatrix}$ represents a rotation through 90° in a clockwise sense (Fig. 21.5). The matrix $\mathbf{R}^2 = \begin{pmatrix} -1 & 0 \\ 0 & -1 \end{pmatrix}$ represents a rotation through 180° in a clockwise sense, and $\mathbf{R}^3 = \begin{pmatrix} 0 & -1 \\ 1 & 0 \end{pmatrix}$ a rotation through 270° in the same sense.

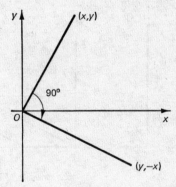

Fig. 21.5

Enlargement

Since $\begin{pmatrix} k & 0 \\ 0 & 1 \end{pmatrix}\begin{pmatrix} x \\ y \end{pmatrix} = \begin{pmatrix} kx \\ y \end{pmatrix}$ this matrix describes a stretching parallel to the x-axis (Fig. 21.6a), and $\begin{pmatrix} 1 & 0 \\ 0 & k \end{pmatrix}$ a stretching parallel to the y-axis (Fig. 21.6b).

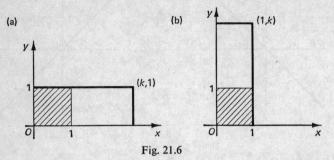

Fig. 21.6

The matrix $\begin{pmatrix} k & 0 \\ 0 & k \end{pmatrix}$ describes an enlargement, centre (0, 0), factor k.

Shear

Since $\begin{pmatrix} 1 & k \\ 0 & 1 \end{pmatrix}\begin{pmatrix} 0 & 1 & 1 & 0 \\ 0 & 0 & 1 & 1 \end{pmatrix} = \begin{pmatrix} 0 & 1 & 1+k & k \\ 0 & 0 & 1 & 1 \end{pmatrix}$ the matrix $\begin{pmatrix} 1 & k \\ 0 & 1 \end{pmatrix}$

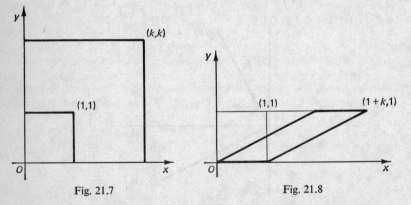

Fig. 21.7   Fig. 21.8

maps the unit square into a paralleogram (Fig. 21.8); such a transformation is called a shear parallel to the x-axis. Similarly $\begin{pmatrix} 1 & 0 \\ k & 1 \end{pmatrix}$ describes a shear parallel to the y-axis.

Mapping of a singular matrix

Any singular matrix can be written $\begin{pmatrix} a & b \\ ka & kb \end{pmatrix}$, and maps the unit square into $(0, 0)$, (a, ka), (b, kb), $(a + b,\ ka + kb)$. These points

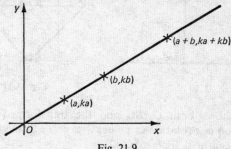

Fig. 21.9

lie on the straight line whose equation is $y = kx$, and the matrix maps the unit square into a line-segment.

Change of area

It can be shown that the ratio of the area of the transformed region to that of the original region is always $D:1$, where D is the value of the determinant of the matrix that describes the transformation. Notice that the determinant of a singular matrix is zero, and the area of the line-segment on to which it maps the unit square is obviously zero.

Example 21.1 *Plot the points whose vertices are described by the matrix* $\begin{pmatrix} 0 & 2 & 2 & 0 \\ 0 & 0 & 2 & 2 \end{pmatrix}$. *Find the figure into which OABC is mapped by the matrix* $\begin{pmatrix} 1 & 1 \\ -1 & 1 \end{pmatrix}$. *Describe the transformation, and find the ratio of the area of the figure OABC to that of the transformed figure OA'B'C'.*

The points whose coordinates are given by the matrix are plotted in Fig. 21.10. Since $\begin{pmatrix} 1 & 1 \\ -1 & 1 \end{pmatrix}\begin{pmatrix} 0 & 2 & 2 & 0 \\ 0 & 0 & 2 & 2 \end{pmatrix} = \begin{pmatrix} 0 & 2 & 4 & 2 \\ 0 & -2 & 0 & 2 \end{pmatrix}$

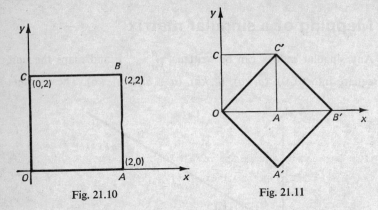

Fig. 21.10   Fig. 21.11

Fig. 21.11 shows both *OABC* and the transformed figure. The transformation is a rotation in a clockwise sense through 45° and an enlargement centre (0, 0), factor $\sqrt{2}$.

Since all lengths are enlarged by a factor $\sqrt{2}$, the area is enlarged by a factor 2, so the ratio of the old area to the new is 1:2. Notice also that the determinant of $\begin{pmatrix} 1 & -1 \\ 1 & 1 \end{pmatrix}$ is 2.

Exercise 21

1 Which of the following matrices represents

(a) a rotation about the origin of 90° in a clockwise sense,

(b) a rotation about the origin of 90° in an anti-clockwise sense?

(i) $\begin{pmatrix} 1 & 0 \\ 0 & -1 \end{pmatrix}$ (ii) $\begin{pmatrix} 0 & -1 \\ 1 & 0 \end{pmatrix}$ (iii) $\begin{pmatrix} 0 & -1 \\ -1 & 0 \end{pmatrix}$

(iv) $\begin{pmatrix} -1 & 0 \\ 0 & 1 \end{pmatrix}$ (v) $\begin{pmatrix} 0 & 1 \\ -1 & 0 \end{pmatrix}$

2 Which of the following matrices represents an enlargement, centre (0, 0), scale factor 4?

(i) $\begin{pmatrix} 2 & 0 \\ 0 & 2 \end{pmatrix}$ (ii) $\begin{pmatrix} 4 & 0 \\ 0 & 4 \end{pmatrix}$ (iii) $\begin{pmatrix} 4 & 0 \\ 0 & 1 \end{pmatrix}$ (iv) $\begin{pmatrix} 4 & 0 \\ 0 & -4 \end{pmatrix}$ (v) $\begin{pmatrix} 2 & 0 \\ 0 & -2 \end{pmatrix}$

3 If $S = \begin{pmatrix} 1 & 0 \\ 3 & 1 \end{pmatrix}$, find the transformation made by **S** on the unit square.

If $R = \begin{pmatrix} 0 & -1 \\ -1 & 0 \end{pmatrix}$, find the matrix **T** given by **R S R** and describe the transformation it represents.

4 The vertices of a square side 5 units are given by the matrix
$\begin{pmatrix} 0 & 5 & 5 & 0 \\ 0 & 0 & 5 & 5 \end{pmatrix}$. Find the transformation made on this square by
the matrix $\begin{pmatrix} 0.6 & 0.8 \\ -0.8 & 0.6 \end{pmatrix}$ by drawing the original square and the
figure into which it is transformed, and using geometrical instruments
to make any necessary measurements.

5 On graph paper mark the points whose coordinates are given by the
matrix **T**, where

$$\mathbf{T} = \begin{pmatrix} 1 & 3 & 5 \\ 1 & 2 & 2 \end{pmatrix}.$$

Join the points to form a triangle T. The triangle T is transformed
into a triangle U by means of the matrix $\mathbf{P} = \begin{pmatrix} 0 & 1 \\ -1 & 0 \end{pmatrix}$ and T is also
transformed into the triangle V by the matrix $\mathbf{Q} = \begin{pmatrix} 1 & 1 \\ 0 & 1 \end{pmatrix}$. Mark
these triangles on the graph paper and describe the geometrical trans-
formations as precisely as possible.

   On another sheet of graph paper, draw the triangle T again, and find
the transformations represented by the matrices $\mathbf{P}^{-1}$ and $\mathbf{Q}^{-1}$.

22 Vectors

Notes on vectors

Vectors are physical quantities having magnitude and direction, combined according to certain laws. Examples of vectors are displacement, velocity, acceleration, force, and momentum. Scalar quantities can be described by a number alone. Examples of scalars are length, area, time, mass, temperature.

A vector in two dimensions, components x and y, can be represented by $x\mathbf{i} + y\mathbf{j}$ or by a column matrix $\begin{pmatrix} x \\ y \end{pmatrix}$ or sometimes by a row matrix $(x\ y)$. The magnitude of this vector is $\sqrt{x^2 + y^2}$.

Addition of vectors

We add vectors by completing a parallelogram as shown (Fig. 22.1). This is equivalent to adding the components, e.g.,

$$\begin{pmatrix} a \\ b \end{pmatrix} + \begin{pmatrix} c \\ d \end{pmatrix} = \begin{pmatrix} a + c \\ b + d \end{pmatrix}$$

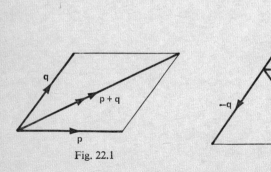

Fig. 22.1   Fig. 22.2

Subtraction of vectors

To subtract **q** from **p**, we add −**q** to **p**. This is equivalent to subtracting the components, e.g.

$$\binom{a}{b} - \binom{c}{d} = \binom{a-c}{b-d}.$$

Vector geometry

If points A, B have position vectors **a**, **b** relative to an origin O, the vector $\overrightarrow{AB} = \mathbf{b} - \mathbf{a}$ (Fig. 22.3a). The position vector of the mid-point M of AB relative to O is $\frac{1}{2}(\mathbf{a} + \mathbf{b})$ (Fig. 22.3b).

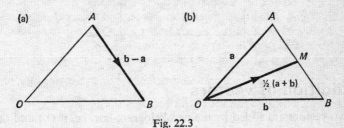

Fig. 22.3

Definition

A vector can be defined as a physical quantity having magnitude and direction, and subject to certain laws of composition. The only law that we define at present is addition.

Displacement vectors

The simplest vectors to consider are displacement vectors, describing the position of one point relative to another. If we start at an origin O, we can travel 4 units in one direction then 3 units at right angles to the first direction as in Fig. 22.1, and arrive at a point P. We can denote the vector that describes the displacement of P from O by $\overrightarrow{OP}$, or by a single letter, say **p**. The displacements 4 and 3 along each of the axes we call the components of **p** along Ox and Oy, and we can write them in terms of unit vectors **i** and **j** along Ox and Oy respectively, or as entries in a column matrix, or occasionally as entries in a row matrix,

i.e. $$\overrightarrow{OP} = \mathbf{p} = 4\mathbf{i} + 3\mathbf{j} = \begin{pmatrix} 4 \\ 3 \end{pmatrix} = (4 \quad 3)$$

The last form is easily confused with coordinates, and should be avoided.

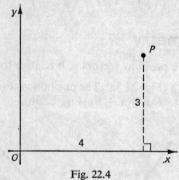

Fig. 22.4

Addition of vectors

Two vectors are added by the parallelogram law, i.e. if $\overrightarrow{OA}$ and $\overrightarrow{OB}$ are two vectors acting through a point O, then their sum $\overrightarrow{OA} + \overrightarrow{OB}$

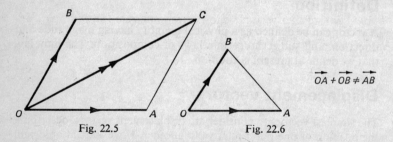

Fig. 22.5   Fig. 22.6

is a vector $\overrightarrow{OC}$, also through O, where OC is the diagonal through O of the parallelogram, two of whose sides are OA and OB. The parallelogram law of addition is the same as that sometimes described as the triangle law, but is much safer; it avoids the danger of thinking that $\overrightarrow{OA} + \overrightarrow{OB} = \overrightarrow{AB}$, using the third side of the triangle.

Addition of components

If two vectors are given in terms of their components, say $\begin{pmatrix} a \\ b \end{pmatrix}$ and $\begin{pmatrix} c \\ d \end{pmatrix}$, then we can define the sum of the vectors by $\begin{pmatrix} a \\ b \end{pmatrix} + \begin{pmatrix} c \\ d \end{pmatrix} = \begin{pmatrix} a + c \\ b + d \end{pmatrix}$. This definition can be extended to three (or more) dimensions. Figure 22.7 shows that for two dimensions the two definitions, addition using the parallelogram rule and addition of components are the same.

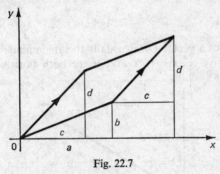

Fig. 22.7

Subtraction of vectors

Subtraction of two vectors follows from our rule for addition, for $\overrightarrow{OA} - \overrightarrow{OB} = \overrightarrow{OA} + (-\overrightarrow{OB})$, as illustrated in Fig. 22.8. Again, if

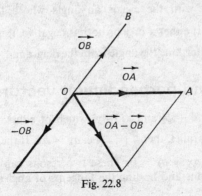

Fig. 22.8

vectors are given in terms of their components, we subtract the components, e.g. $\begin{pmatrix} a \\ b \end{pmatrix} - \begin{pmatrix} c \\ d \end{pmatrix} = \begin{pmatrix} a - c \\ b - d \end{pmatrix}$

Magnitude of a vector

If a vector is given in terms of its components, $x\mathbf{i} + y\mathbf{j}$ or $\begin{pmatrix} x \\ y \end{pmatrix}$, then the magnitude of the vector written $|x\mathbf{i} + y\mathbf{j}|$ is $\sqrt{(x^2 + y^2)}$. Thus in Fig. 22.4, the magnitude of the vector $4\mathbf{i} + 3\mathbf{j} = \sqrt{4^2 + 3^2}$, i.e. 5, which is the length of the line OP.

Direction

The direction of a vector OP is usually the angle made by the vector with the positive x-axis. If x and y are both positive, the vector

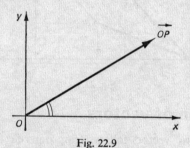

Fig. 22.9

$x\mathbf{i} + y\mathbf{j}$ makes with the x-axis an angle whose tangent is $\left(\dfrac{y}{x}\right)$, i.e. $\tan^{-1}\left(\dfrac{y}{x}\right)$. If either x or y or both is negative, it is best to draw a diagram and determine the angle from the diagram.

Parallel and perpendicular vectors

If two vectors $a\mathbf{i} + b\mathbf{j}$ and $x\mathbf{i} + y\mathbf{j}$ which of course can be written $\begin{pmatrix} a \\ b \end{pmatrix}$, $\begin{pmatrix} x \\ y \end{pmatrix}$ are parallel, then $\dfrac{a}{b} = \dfrac{x}{y}$, i.e. $ay = bx$. If the two vectors are perpendicular, $ax + by = 0$. These two results can be obtained by drawing diagrams and finding the tangents of angles that are equal.

Example 22.1 *Note the following results.*

(a) $\begin{pmatrix} 2 \\ 4 \end{pmatrix} + \begin{pmatrix} 3 \\ 1 \end{pmatrix} = \begin{pmatrix} 5 \\ 5 \end{pmatrix}$ and $\begin{pmatrix} 2 \\ 4 \end{pmatrix} - \begin{pmatrix} 3 \\ 1 \end{pmatrix} = \begin{pmatrix} -1 \\ 3 \end{pmatrix}$

This can also be written $(2\mathbf{i} + 4\mathbf{j}) + (3\mathbf{i} + \mathbf{j}) = 5\mathbf{i} + 5\mathbf{j}$,

and $(2\mathbf{i} + 4\mathbf{j}) - (3\mathbf{i} + \mathbf{j}) = -\mathbf{i} + 3\mathbf{j}$.

(b) $2 \begin{pmatrix} 2 \\ 3 \end{pmatrix} = \begin{pmatrix} 4 \\ 6 \end{pmatrix}$ and $\frac{1}{2} \begin{pmatrix} 2 \\ 3 \end{pmatrix} = \begin{pmatrix} 1 \\ 1\frac{1}{2} \end{pmatrix}$

(c) *The magnitude of the vector* $\begin{pmatrix} 2 \\ 3 \end{pmatrix}$ *is* $\sqrt{2^2 + 3^2}$, *i.e.* $\sqrt{13}$.

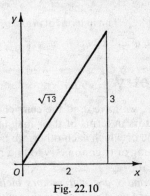

Fig. 22.10

The angle it makes with the x-axis is $\tan^{-1}(3/2)$

(d) *If the vectors* $\begin{pmatrix} 2 \\ 3 \end{pmatrix}$ *and* $\begin{pmatrix} k \\ 6 \end{pmatrix}$ *are parallel, then* $\frac{2}{3} = \frac{k}{6}$, *so* $k = 4$.

(e) *If the vectors* $\begin{pmatrix} 2 \\ 3 \end{pmatrix}$ *and* $\begin{pmatrix} k \\ 6 \end{pmatrix}$ *are perpendicular then* $2k + 3 \times 6 = 0$, *i.e.* $k = -9$. *The vector perpendicular to* $\begin{pmatrix} 2 \\ 3 \end{pmatrix}$ *is* $\begin{pmatrix} -9 \\ 6 \end{pmatrix}$.

Exercise 22a

1 On graph paper, draw a pair of coordinate axes. Mark the points whose coordinates are O (0, 0), A (2, 3), B (3, 5), and C (4, 2). Write down the position vectors of

(a) A relative to O, i.e. $\overrightarrow{OA}$, (b) B relative to O, i.e. $\overrightarrow{OB}$,

(c) A relative to B, i.e. $\overrightarrow{BA}$, (d) B relative to A, i.e. $\overrightarrow{AB}$,

(e) C relative to B, i.e. $\overrightarrow{BC}$.

2 Find the magnitude of each of the following vectors, and the angle it makes with the positive x-axis.

(a) $\begin{pmatrix} 2 \\ 2 \end{pmatrix}$ (b) $\begin{pmatrix} 3 \\ -3 \end{pmatrix}$ (c) $\begin{pmatrix} -1 \\ 1 \end{pmatrix}$ (iv) $\begin{pmatrix} -2 \\ -2 \end{pmatrix}$

3 If $\mathbf{a} = \begin{pmatrix} 2 \\ -1 \end{pmatrix}$, $\mathbf{b} = \begin{pmatrix} 3 \\ 2 \end{pmatrix}$, and $\mathbf{c} = \begin{pmatrix} 4 \\ 0 \end{pmatrix}$ find the magnitude of

(a) $\mathbf{a} + \mathbf{b}$ (b) $\mathbf{a} - \mathbf{c}$

(c) $\mathbf{a} + 2\mathbf{b}$ (d) $2\mathbf{a} - \mathbf{c}$ (e) $\mathbf{a} + \mathbf{b} + \mathbf{c}$

4 If $\begin{pmatrix} a \\ 3 \end{pmatrix}$ is parallel to $\begin{pmatrix} -1 \\ -6 \end{pmatrix}$, find a.

5 If $\begin{pmatrix} a \\ 3 \end{pmatrix}$ is perpendicular to $\begin{pmatrix} 6 \\ 1 \end{pmatrix}$, find a.

6 If $\mathbf{a} = \begin{pmatrix} 3 \\ 1 \end{pmatrix}$ and $\mathbf{b} = \begin{pmatrix} -1 \\ 2 \end{pmatrix}$, find in terms of m and n, the vector $m\mathbf{a} + n\mathbf{b}$. Hence find m and n if $m\mathbf{a} + n\mathbf{b} = \begin{pmatrix} 8 \\ 19 \end{pmatrix}$.

Use of geometry

In all these examples, we have used the **components** of the vector. If we are given the vectors in terms of their magnitudes and directions made with a fixed line or which each other, we have to use geometry, and either scale drawing or trigonometry to find resultants, etc.

Example 22.2 *If* **u** *and* **v** *are unit vectors inclined at* 20°, *find the magnitude of* **u** + **v**, *and the direction it makes with the vector* **u**.

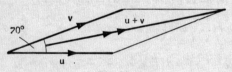

Fig. 22.11

Fig. 22.11 shows the parallelogram that enables us to see the vector **u** + **v**. Since the parallelogram is a rhombus, $|\mathbf{u} + \mathbf{v}| = 2 \cos 10°$ = 1.97. The angle it makes with the vector **u** is clearly 10°.

Example 22.3 *If* **u** *and* **v** *are unit vectors inclined at* 40°, *find the magnitude of* **u** − 2**v**, *and the angle it makes with the vector* **u**.

We can solve this problem by making a scale drawing, as in Fig. 22.12, from which we can read that $|\mathbf{u} - 2\mathbf{v}|$ is 1.4, and the angle it makes with **u** is 112°. To solve the problem by calculation, it is

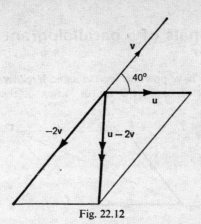

Fig. 22.12

necessary to use the cosine formula and then the sine formula, beginning $x^2 = 1^2 + 2^2 - 2 \times 1 \times 2 \cos 40°$, where $x = |\mathbf{u} - 2\mathbf{v}|$.

Exercise 22b

1 The angle between two unit vectors $\mathbf{p}$ and $\mathbf{q}$ is 60°. Calculate
   (a) $|\mathbf{p} - \mathbf{q}|$, (b) $|\mathbf{p} + \mathbf{q}|$.
2 The angle between two unit vectors $\mathbf{p}$ and $\mathbf{q}$ is 30°. Calculate the angle made with $\mathbf{p}$ by (a) $\mathbf{p} - \mathbf{q}$, (b) $\mathbf{p} + \mathbf{q}$.
3 Two unit vectors $\mathbf{u}$ and $\mathbf{v}$ are inclined at 50°. Find $|\mathbf{u} + \mathbf{v}|$ and the angle made by $\mathbf{u} + \mathbf{v}$ with the vector $\mathbf{u}$.
4 If $\mathbf{u}$ and $\mathbf{v}$ are unit vectors, find the angle between them if $|\mathbf{u} - \mathbf{v}| = 1.6$.
5 If $\mathbf{u}$ and $\mathbf{v}$ are unit vectors inclined at 60°, find (a) $|\mathbf{u} + 2\mathbf{v}|$, (b) the angle between $\mathbf{u} + 2\mathbf{v}$ and the vector $\mathbf{u}$.

Geometrical applications

With the usual notation, we see in Fig. 22.13 that if $\overrightarrow{OB} = \overrightarrow{OA} + \overrightarrow{AB}$
$\overrightarrow{AB} = \overrightarrow{OB} - \overrightarrow{OA}$, i.e. $\overrightarrow{AB} = b - a$, where $\overrightarrow{OB} = b, \overrightarrow{OA} - a$.

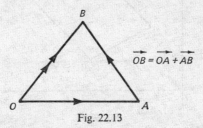

$\overrightarrow{OB} = \overrightarrow{OA} + \overrightarrow{AB}$

Fig. 22.13

The diagonals of a parallelogram bisect each other

Let points A, B have position vectors **a** and **b** relative to O. Then the position of vector of C, the fourth vertex of the parallelogram,

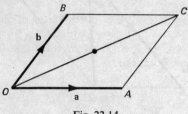

Fig. 22.14

$OACB$ is $\mathbf{a} + \mathbf{b}$ and the position vector of the mid-point of OC is $\frac{1}{2}(\mathbf{a} + \mathbf{b})$. The vector describing the displacement AB is $(\mathbf{b} - \mathbf{a})$, and so the vector describing half that displacement is $\frac{1}{2}(\mathbf{b} - \mathbf{a})$; thus the position vector relative to O of the mid point of BA is $\mathbf{a} + \frac{1}{2}(\mathbf{b} - \mathbf{a})$ i.e. $\frac{1}{2}(\mathbf{b} + \mathbf{a})$. Since the midpoints of the two diagonals have the same position vectors relative to the origin O, they must be the same points, i.e. the diagonals of a parallelogram besect each other.

Example 22.4 *If the position vectors of points A, B and C relative to an origin O are* $(1, 2)$, $(3, 1)$, *and* $(5, 3)$ *respectively, find the fourth vertex of the parallelogram $ABCD$.*

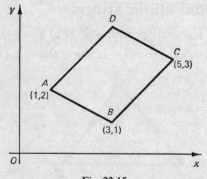

Fig. 22.15

The displacement vector $\overrightarrow{AD}$ must be equal to the displacement vector $\overrightarrow{BC}$.

But $$\overrightarrow{BC} = \begin{pmatrix} 5 \\ 3 \end{pmatrix} - \begin{pmatrix} 3 \\ 1 \end{pmatrix} = \begin{pmatrix} 2 \\ 2 \end{pmatrix} \quad \therefore \overrightarrow{AD} = \begin{pmatrix} 2 \\ 2 \end{pmatrix}$$

But $\overrightarrow{OD} = \overrightarrow{OA} + \overrightarrow{AD} = \begin{pmatrix} 1 \\ 2 \end{pmatrix} + \begin{pmatrix} 2 \\ 2 \end{pmatrix} = \begin{pmatrix} 3 \\ 4 \end{pmatrix}$

Therefore the coordinates of the fourth vertex of the parallelogram $ABCD$ are (3, 4). Notice that if we had required the fourth vertex of the parallelogram $ABDC$, it is (7, 2). We must take care to draw the correct figure in these questions.

Exercise 22c

1 If the position vectors of points A and B relative to an origin O are **a** and **b**, write down the vector $\overrightarrow{BA}$. Write down the position vectors of X and Y, the midpoints of OA and OB. Find the vector $\overrightarrow{YX}$. Deduce a relation between the lengths of AB and XY, and the directions of AB and XY.

2 With the data of question 1, P and Q are points on OA and OB such that $OP = \frac{1}{3} OA$, $OQ = \frac{1}{3} OB$. Use the method of question 1 to find $PQ : AB$.

3 If the position vectors relative to an origin O of points A, B and C are **a**, **b**, and **c** respectively, find the position vector of A', the midpoint of BC, and the position vector of the point L in AA' such that $AL = \frac{2}{3} AA'$. If B' is the midpoint of AC, and M is the point in BB' such that $BM = \frac{2}{3} BB'$, find the position vector of M. The point N is defined in a similar way. Deduce that the medians of a triangle intersect in a point.

4 If the position vectors of points A, B, and C are $\begin{pmatrix} 1 \\ 5 \end{pmatrix}$, $\begin{pmatrix} 3 \\ 1 \end{pmatrix}$, $\begin{pmatrix} 7 \\ 3 \end{pmatrix}$, respectively, find the fourth vertex of the parallelogram $ABCD$. Use Pythagoras' theorem to prove that this parallelogram is a square.

5 In the parallelogram $OABC$, the line OA is produced to D so that A is the midpoint of OD. The point E on OC is such that $OE = 2OC$. Prove that E lies on BD. (*Hint:* let the position vectors of A and B be **a** and **b** respectively. Write down the position vector of C and then of E. Find the vectors BE and BD.)

23 Calculus

Notes

Differentiating

If $y = x^n, \dfrac{dy}{dx} = nx^{n-}$.

N.B. the differential coefficient of a constant is zero.

Integrating

$$\text{If } \frac{dy}{dx} = x^n, y = \frac{1}{n+1} x^{n+1} + c. \, n \neq -1$$

Area

The area of the region bounded by the curve $y = f(x)$, the x-axis and the lines $x = a, x = b$ is $\displaystyle\int_a^b y \, dx$.

The area of the region bounded by the curve $x = f(y)$, the y-axis and the lines $y = c, y = d$ is $\displaystyle\int_c^d x \, dy$.

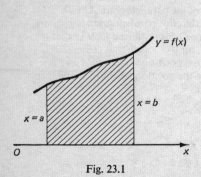

Fig. 23.1   Fig. 23.2

Volume of solid of revolution

The volume of the solid obtained by rotating completely about the x-axis the region bounded by $y = f(x)$, the x-axis and the lines

$x = a, x = b$, is $\pi \int_a^b y^2 \, dx$.

The volume of the solid obtained by rotating completely about

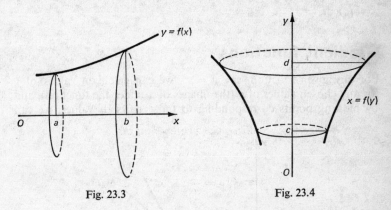

Fig. 23.3   Fig. 23.4

the y-axis the region bounded by the curve $x = f(y)$, the y-axis and

the lines $y = c, y = d$, is $\pi \int_c^d x^2 \, dy$.

Maxima and minima

At a maximum point (P) on a curve, $\dfrac{dy}{dx} = 0$ and is decreasing positive, zero, then negative. At a minimum point (Q), $\dfrac{dy}{dx} = 0$ and is increasing negative, zero, positive.

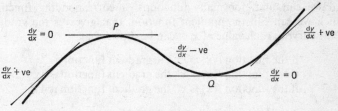

Fig. 23.5

Displacement, velocity, and acceleration

If the displacement s metres of a body travelling in a straight line is given at time t seconds as a function of t, then the velocity v m s^{-1} is given by $v = \dfrac{ds}{dt}$, and the acceleration a m s^{-2} is given by $a = \dfrac{dv}{dt}$.

If the acceleration a m s^{-2} of a body travelling in a straight line is given at time t seconds as a function of t, then the velocity v m s^{-1} is given by $v = \int a\, dt$, and the displacement s metres is given by $s = \int v\, dt$.

Gradient functions

For any given function, say $y = x^2$, we can calculate values of y for any chosen values of x (the images of x under the function), and by plotting points corresponding to those pairs of values, we can

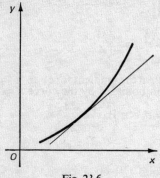

Fig. 23.6

obtain a curve we describe as the graph of that function. The gradient of the curve at any point is the gradient of the tangent at that point, and we can find, for many functions, a corresponding function, which we can call the gradient function, that gives us the gradient of the curve at each value of x. It can be shown that

> if the function $f(x)$ is x^2, the gradient function is $2x$
> if the function $f(x)$ is x^3, the gradient function is $3x^2$
> if the function $f(x)$ is x^4, the gradient function is $4x^3$

so   if the function is x^n, the gradient function is nx^{n-1}.

If the function is $ax^3 + bx^2 + cx + d$, the gradient function is $3ax^2 + 2bx + c$. Notice that the gradient function of a constant is zero. This process of finding the gradient function is called differentiating, and the gradient function is more precisely called the derived function. If the function is denoted by y, the derived function is written $\dfrac{dy}{dx}$: if the function is denoted by f, the derived function is written f'.

Example 23.1 *Find the gradient at the point at which $x = 2$ of the curve for which $y = 3x^2 - 6x - 4$.*

Since the function is $3x^2 - 6x - 4$, the gradient function is $6x - 6$. Thus when $x = 2$, the gradient of the curve is 6.

Example 23.2 *Find the point on the curve $y = 3x^2 - 6x - 4$ at which the gradient is 0.*

Since the gradient function is $6x - 6$, we need to solve $6x - 6 = 0$, i.e. $x = 1$. Therefore the point is $(1, -7)$, substituting $x = 1$ in the equation of the curve.

Example 23.3 *If $y = \dfrac{4}{x}$, find $\dfrac{dy}{dx}$.*

Write $\dfrac{4}{x}$ as $4(x^{-1})$. Then the gradient function is $4(-1)(x^{-2})$, i.e.

$$\frac{dy}{dx} = -4x^{-2}$$
$$= \frac{-4}{x^2}.$$

Exercise 23a

1 Find the derived function of each of the following functions:

(a) $4x^3$ (b) $5x^4 + 3x$ (c) $5x^4 + 3$

(d) $6x + \dfrac{1}{x}$ (e) $6 - \dfrac{2}{x^3}$ (f) $2x^2 - \dfrac{1}{x^4}$

2 Find the gradient of the curve $y = 4x - x^2$ when $x = 1$, and the co-ordinates of the point on the curve at which the gradient is 0.

Integration

The inverse process of differentiation, finding the original function if we know the derived function, is called integration. One difficulty which can arise is because the derived function of a constant is zero, so that if the derived function is known to be $3x^2 + 2x + 1$, then the original function may have been $x^3 + x^2 + x$ or $x^3 + x^2 + x + 1$ or $x^3 + x^2 + x + 21$ or $x^3 + x^2 + x + C$, for any value of the constant C. We may have some additional information, but if we do not, then we should always put in an arbitrary constant C.

If the function $y = x^n$, the derived function $\dfrac{dy}{dx} = nx^{n-1}$ so if

the derived function is $\qquad \dfrac{dy}{dx} = x^n,$

the original function $\quad y = \dfrac{1}{n+1}\, x^{n+1} + C.$

Example 23.4 *Find y if* $\dfrac{dy}{dx} = 6x^2 + 2x + 4$

Applying the rule above, $y = 2x^3 + x^2 + 4x + C.$

Example 23.5 *If* $\dfrac{dy}{dx} = 2 + \dfrac{1}{x^2}$ *and* $y = 2$ *when* $x = 1$, *find y in terms of x.*

Write $\dfrac{1}{x^2}$ as x^{-2}. Then as $\dfrac{dy}{dx} = 2 + \dfrac{1}{x^2}$

$$y = 2x - x^{-1} + C.$$

But when $x = 1$, $y = 2$, so that $2 = 2 - 1 + C$, i.e. $C = 1$, so $y = 2x - \dfrac{1}{x} + 1.$

Area of a region between a curve and the x-axis

The integral of a function of x with respect to x is written $\int y\, dx.$

It can be shown that the exact value of the area of the region bounded by the curve whose equation is $y = f(x)$, the lines $x = a$ and $x = b$ and the x-axis is $\int_a^b y\, dx$ where $\int_a^b$ is interpreted as in Example 23.6 (Fig 23.7).

Example 23.6 *Find the area of the region bounded by the curve* $y = 3x^2 + 1$, *the lines* $x = -1$ *and* $x = 2$ *and the x-axis.*

Always draw a diagram to show the region whose area we are finding.

$$\text{Then the area} = \int_{-1}^{3} (3x^2 + 1)\, dx$$

$$= [x^3 + x]_{-1}^{3}$$

The limits of the integral, 3 and −1, mean that we evaluate the integral first when $x = 3$, then subtract from this the value when

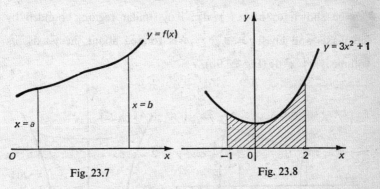

Fig. 23.7   Fig. 23.8

$x = -1$. Thus the area of the region is $(3)^3 + 3 - \{(-1)^3 - 1\}$ i.e. 32 square units.

If the area of the region is negative, the region lies below the x-axis. Sketching the curve and identifying the region helps to reduce errors.

Exercise 23b

1 Find the integrals of each of the following:

(a) x^2 (b) $4x^3$ (c) $7x^6$ (d) $6x^6$

(e) $4x^3 + 3x^2$ (f) $3x^2 + \dfrac{1}{x^2}$ (g) $3 + \dfrac{1}{x^2}$ (h) $2x - \dfrac{2}{x^2}$

(i) $3x^1 + \dfrac{3}{x^4}$ (j) $4x^3 - \dfrac{4}{x^3}$

2 Find y, if $\dfrac{dy}{dx}$ equals

(a) $2x + 3$ (b) $4x^3 + 3x^2 + 2x$ (c) $\dfrac{1}{x^2} + \dfrac{1}{x^3}$

3 Find y if $\dfrac{dy}{dx} = 3x^2 + 2x + 1$ and $y = 2$ when $x = 1$.

4 Find the area of the region bounded by the curve $y = 3x^2 + 2x$, the x-axis and the lines $x = 3$ and $x = 1$.

5 Find the area of the region bounded by the curve $y = \dfrac{1}{x^2}$, the x-axis and the lines $x = 1$ and $x = 2$.

Volumes of solids of revolution

If a plane region, bounded by the curve $y = f(x)$, ordinates $x = a$ and $x = b$ and the x-axis, is rotated about the x-axis, its volume can be shown to be $\pi \displaystyle\int_a^b y^2 \, dx$: if a similar region, bounded by the y-axis and lines $y = c$, $y = d$ is rotated about the y-axis, its volume is $\pi \displaystyle\int_c^d x^2 \, dy$ (Fig. 23.9b).

(a)   (b)

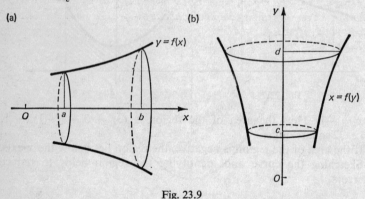

Fig. 23.9

Example 23.7 *Find the volume of the solid formed by rotating about the x-axis the region bounded by $y = x^2$, $x = 1$, $x = 2$ and the x-axis.*

The region and the solid are shown in Fig. 23.10. The volume V is given by

$$V = \pi \int_1^2 y^2 \, dx$$
$$= \pi \int_1^2 x^4 \, dx$$
$$= \pi [\tfrac{1}{5} x^5]_1^2$$
$$= \tfrac{31}{5} \pi, \text{ i.e. } 6\tfrac{1}{5} \pi.$$

Check The solid formed is nearly a cone, with base radius 4, height 1, so we expect the volume to be about $\frac{1}{3}\pi(4)^2$, about $5\frac{1}{3}\pi$.

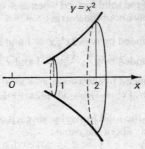

Fig. 23.10

Example 23.8 *The region bounded by the curve $y = x^2$, $y = 1$, $y = 2$ and the y-axis is rotated completely about the y-axis. Find the volume of the solid formed.*

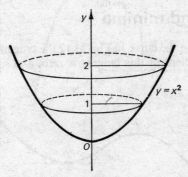

Fig. 23.11

The volume V is given by $V = \pi \displaystyle\int_1^2 x^2 \, dy$. Since we are to integrate

with respect to y, we must write the equation of the curve $y = x^2$ as $x = y^{\frac{1}{2}}$, and the limits must be the values of y we were given. Thus

$$V = \pi \int_1^2 (y^{\frac{1}{2}})^2 \, dy$$
$$= \pi[\tfrac{1}{2}y^2]_1^2$$
$$= \tfrac{3}{2}\pi$$

Exercise 23c

1 Find the volume of the solid formed when each of the following regions is rotated completely about the x-axis.

  (a) The region bounded by $y = 3x^4$, $x = 1$ and $x = 2$, and the x-axis.

  (b) The region bounded by $y = \dfrac{1}{x}$, $x = 1$ and $x = 2$, and the x-axis.

  (c) The region bounded by the x-axis, $y = x^2 + 1$, $x = 1$, and the y-axis. (*Hint:* $(x^2 + 1)^2 = x^4 + 2x^2 + 1$.)

2 Find the volume of the solid formed when each of the following regions is rotated completely about the y-axis:

  (a) The region bounded by $y = \dfrac{1}{x}$, $y = 1$, $y = 2$, and the y-axis.

  (b) The region bounded by $x = y^2$, $y = 3$, and the y-axis.

  (c) The region bounded by $y = x^2$, $y = 3$, and the y-axis.

Maxima and minima

At the point P on the curve in Fig. 23.12 the tangent is parallel to the x-axis. The gradient of this tangent is zero, and so the value of the

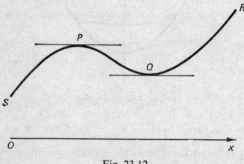

Fig. 23.12

derived function is zero. The gradient is first positive then negative on either side of P; such a point is called a **maximum**. The value of y at P is greater than the value of y at points either side of P, but is not necessarily the greatest value of all. At the point R, for example, the value of y is clearly greater than at P.

At the point Q the gradient is also zero. Here the value of y is less than at the points either side, though again it is not necessarily the least value on the curve; the value of y at S is clearly less than at Q. The point Q is called a **minimum**. Just before Q, the gradient is negative; just after Q the gradient is positive.

N.B. *At a maximum, the gradient is zero, and changes from positive to negative.*

At a minimum, the gradient is zero and changes from negative to positive.

Example 23.9 *Find the maximum and minimum points on the curve whose equation is $y = x^3 + x^2 - x$, distinguishing between them.*

Since
$$y = x^3 + x^2 - x$$
$$\frac{dy}{dx} = 3x^2 + 2x - 1$$
$$= (3x - 1)(x + 1)$$

so the gradient $= 0$ when $x = \frac{1}{3}$ or -1.

When x is less than -1, say $x = -2$, $\frac{dy}{dx} = (-7)(-1)$, positive.

When x is a little greater than -1, say $x = 0$, $\frac{dy}{dx}$ is negative.

The gradient is thus positive, zero, negative, so that $x = -1$ gives a maximum.

When x is a little less than $\frac{1}{3}$, say $x = 0$, we already know that the gradient is negative: when x is greater than $\frac{1}{3}$, say $x = 1$, the gradient is positive, so that the gradient is negative, zero, positive, and $x = \frac{1}{3}$ is a minimum.

To find the maximum *value*, we must find the value of y when $x = -1$, that is, $y = (-1)^3 + (-1)^2 - (-1)$, i.e. $y = 1$: to find the minimum value, $y = \frac{-5}{27}$. The maximum and minimum points are therefore max $(-1, 1)$: min $\left(\frac{1}{3}, \frac{-5}{27} \right)$.

N.B. Note carefully whether the maximum and minimum *points* are required, or whether the maximum and minimum *values* of y are required.

The curve is sketched below.

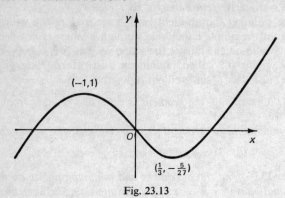

Fig. 23.13

Exercise 23d

1 Find the maximum or minimum values of the following:

(a) $y = 2x^2 - 4x$ (b) $y = 6x - x^2$
(c) $y = x^3 - 3x^2$ (d) $y = x^3 + 2x^2 + x + 1$

2 Find the coordinates of the maximum and minimum points on each of the following:

(a) $y = x^2 + 2x$ (b) $y = 3 - 6x - x^2$
(c) $y = 6x^2 - x^3$ (d) $y = x^3 - 3x - 1$

Velocity and acceleration

The gradient function measures the rate of change of the function. Since velocity is defined as the rate of change of displacement with respect to time, if the displacement s is given as a function of time t, $\dfrac{\mathrm{d}s}{\mathrm{d}t}$ is the velocity function. Similarly, since acceleration is the rate of change of the velocity with respect to time, if the velocity v is given as a function of time t, the acceleration is $\dfrac{\mathrm{d}v}{\mathrm{d}t}$. Knowing the displacement function, by differentiating we can find the velocity function and the acceleration-function. Knowing acceleration (or velocity) and some additional information to find the constant of integration, by integrating we can find the velocity (or displacement) function.

Example 23.10 *The displacement s metres along a fixed line of a body at time t seconds is given by s = t³ + t². Find (a) the velocity initially (b) the velocity after 2 seconds (c) the acceleration after 2 seconds.*

Since $s = t^3 + t^2$, $v = \dfrac{ds}{dt} = 3t^2 + 2t$, so when t = 0 the velocity is zero, and the velocity when $t = 2$ is 16 m s^{-1}.

Since $v = 3t^2 + 2t$, $a = \dfrac{dv}{dt} = 6t + 2$, so that the acceleration after 2 seconds is 14 m s^{-2}.

Example 23.11 *The acceleration a m s^{-2} of a body at time t seconds is given by a = 12t. If the body starts from rest, find its velocity and displacement after 5 s.*

Since $a = 12t$, $\dfrac{dv}{dt} = 12t$, so $v = 6t^2 + C$. But when $t = 0$ and $v = 0, C = 0$, so $v = 6t^2$.

Since $v = 6t^2$, $\dfrac{ds}{dt} = 6t^2$, so $s = 2t^3 + C$. Again, $s = 0$ when $t = 0$, if we measure the displacement from the initial position, so $s = 2t^3$. Thus the velocity after 5 s is 150 m s^{-1} and the displacement is 250 m.

Exercise 23e

1 A body moves in a straight line so that after t seconds its distance from a fixed point O in the line is s metres, where $s = t^3 - 1$.
Find its velocity and acceleration after 1 second.

2 A body moves in a straight line so that after t seconds its distance from a fixed point O in the line is s metres, where $s = t^2 + 5t + 1$.
Find its velocity and acceleration after 2 seconds.

3 A body moves in a straight line so that after t seconds its velocity is v m s^{-1}, where $v = 3t^2 + 2t + 1$. Find its acceleration after 1 second, and its distance from the initial position. Find also its velocity after 2 seconds, and the distance moved in the first 2 seconds.

4 A body moves in a straight line so that after t seconds its acceleration is a m s^{-2}, where $a = 12t^2$. If the body has velocity 1 m s^{-1} when $t = 1$, find its velocity when $t = 2$, and the distance travelled in the first 2 seconds.

Answers

Exercise 1a

1 (a) 101, 111, 1001, 1101, 10 111, 11 000, 110 000, 1 000 000, 1 100 000
  (b) 12, 21, 100, 111, 212, 220, 1210, 2101, 10 120
  (c) 5, 7, 11, 15, 27, 30, 60, 100, 140
  (d) 5, 7, 9, 11, 1e, 20, 40, 54, 80
2 3, 5, 10, 12, 24, 56
3 7, 25, 61, 81, 162   4 3, 7, 10, 30, 100
5 1001, 1 001 001, 1011, 1 000 000, 1 011 111
6 (a) seven (b) eight (c) six
7 Last two digits are 00   8 Last digit is 0 or 4
9 The sum of the digits is divisible by 7
10 (b) 26 (d) $n^3 - 1$

Exercise 1b

1 (a) 0.09 (b) 0.49 (c) 3.5 (d) 35 (e) 0.0035
2 (a) 6.25 (b) 13 3 (a) $\frac{14}{15}$ (b) $1\frac{11}{15}$
4 (a) $2\frac{7}{19}$ (b) $1\frac{5}{8}$
5 (a) 0.01; 0.0001; 0.1001 (b) 0.5; 0.25; 0.375

Exercise 1(c)

1 (a) 7.8×10^2 (b) 6.78×10^5 (c) 8×10^{-3} (d) 1×10^{-1}
2 (a) 6×10^5 (b) 1.5×10^{-1} (c) 1.5×10^5 (d) 1.5×10^1
3 (a) 2×10^{-2} (b) 7.5×10^{-4} 4 0.1, $\frac{2}{15}$, 1.5×10^{-1}

Exercise 2a

1 (a) 16.8 cm² (b) 28 cm² 2 (a) 16 cm (b) 80 cm
3 (a) 1.5 km (b) 4 cm (c) 1 km² (d) 16 cm²
4 (a) 1:20 (b) 1:400 (c) 1:8000

Exercise 2b

1 5300; 5400; 5400; 0.53; 0.50; 0.50
2 5.35; 5.36; 5.36; 5.36; 0.55; 0.56; 0.51; 0.50
3 (a) 48 (b) 72 (c) 0.3 (d) 10

Exercise 3a
1 5:4:2   2 6:3:1   3 3:6:2
4 £1, £1.50, £2.50   5 £1000, £1500, £2000   6 £2.40, £3.60, £6.00

Exercise 3b
1 128   2 800   3 £3000   4 (a) £1.92   (b) £480
5 $\dfrac{100\,y}{x+y}$ 6 £32; £34.56   7 10 944   8 280
9 £2880   10 £2015.50

Exercise 3c
1 £170   2 £9   3 £16   4 (a) £402   (b) £34   (c) £77
5 $3\frac{1}{2}\%$ 6 3 months   7 £1600   8 6%
9 $12\frac{1}{2}\%$ 10 £5400, £4752, £4052.16, £3296.33
11 £2336.26   12 (a) £129 (b) £104 (c) £1275 (d) £980

Exercise 4a
1 $2x(2-3y)$ 2 $2h(2h-3)$ 3 $4y(1-3y)$
4 $x^2(1+3x)$ 5 $x^2(1+x^3)$ 6 $x^2(1+x^4)$
7 $2a^2(1+3a-2b)$ 8 $3x^2(y+1)$ 9 $a^2(a^2+a+1)$
10 $4x^2(1+2x+3x^2+4x^3)$

Exercise 4b
1 $(x-y)(x+y)$ 2 $(p-7q)(p+7q)$
3 $(5a-3b)(5a+3b)$ 4 $2(s-3t)(s+3t)$
5 $4(1-3x)(1+3x)$ 6 $7y(1-3y)(1+3y)$
7 $b(a-c)(a+c)$ 8 $(x-1)(x+1)(x^2+1)$
9 $(a+b-c)(a-b+c)$ 10 $\pi(x-y+z)(x-y-z)$
11 2.2   12 2
13 4000   14 31.4

Exercise 4c
1 $(x+1)(x+6)$ 2 $(x-2)(x-3)$ 3 $(y-3)(y+2)$
4 $(z-6)(z+1)$ 5 $(x-6)(x+2)$ 6 $(4x+1)(x-1)$
7 $(3x+2)(x-1)$ 8 $(3y+2)(y-3)$ 9 $(5+y)(1+y)$
10 $2(2x+5)(x-3)$

Exercise 4d
1 $(a+2)(a+x)$ 2 $(x+2)(y+4)$ 3 $(x+2)(x+y)$
4 $(x-y)(y-z)$ 5 $(x+y)(x-y+1)$ 6 $(x-y)(x+y+1)$
7 $(z+2)(z+1+a)$ 8 $(y+5)(y+2+x)$

Exercise 4e
1 $c(a-b)(a+b)$ 2 $c(a^2-b)$ 3 $ac(a-b)$
4 $(a+b)(b+c)$ 5 $(4a+1)(a-1)$ 6 $(5+4t)(3-t)$
7 $(a-b)(2x-3y)$ 8 $2(3x-5y)(3x+5y)$ 9 $(x+2+10y)(x+2)$
10 $abc\,(a-1)(a+1)$

Exercise 5a

1 7p   **2** 9   **3** 155 at 30p, 55 at 50p.   **4** 15   **5** 490

Exercise 5b

1 $\frac{4}{5}$ **2** $\frac{7}{5}$ **3** 3   **4** -3 **5** $1\frac{8}{5}$
6 3   **7** -9 **8** 9   **9** 8   **10** 1

Exercise 5c

1 $x < 2$ **2** $x < -\frac{2}{3}$ **3** $x > \frac{2}{3}$ **4** $x > 2$
5 $x > -7$ **6** $x > -2$ **7** $x > -2$ **8** $x > 4$
9 $x > 56$ **10** $x \leqslant 27$

Exercise 5d

1 $\frac{17}{13}$, $\frac{2}{13}$ **2** $\frac{4}{11}$, $\frac{19}{11}$ **3** $\frac{9}{2}$, $\frac{3}{4}$ **4** 3, -4
5 120, 80

Exercise 5c

1 4, 4, 0   **2** 1, 0, 1   **3** 3, -1 **4** Identity

Exercise 5f

1 -1 or 6   **2** 2 or 5   **3** -2 or -3 **4** 0 or -5
5 0 or $-\frac{2}{3}$ **6** -1 or $\frac{1}{3}$

Exercise 5g

1 -0.29 or -1.71 **2** -0.22 or 2.22   **3** -2.56 or 1.56
4 -2.64 or 1.14

Exercise 6a

1 (a) $12a^7$ (b) $\frac{4}{3a}$ (c) $7a$ (d) 1

2 (a) 18   (b) 108   (c) 324 (d) 9

Exercise 6b

1 (a) 27   (b) $\frac{1}{3}$ (c) 25   (d) $\frac{1}{6}$ (e) 1   (f) 4   (g) $\frac{1}{8}$ (h) $\frac{1}{81}$
2 (a) a (b) b^2 (c) $a^{\frac{1}{2}}b^{\frac{1}{2}}$ (d) b (e) ab^{-1}

Exercise 6c

1 (a) 2   (b) 3   (c) 3   (d) 3
2 (a) 2.585   (b) 3.322   (c) -0.737 (d) 0.263
   (e) 4.644   (f) 6.229

Exercise 6d

1 (a) $I = kt$ (b) $T = kv^2$ (c) $t = k/\sqrt{n}$ **2** 30.

Exercise 6e

1 (b), (c), (d)   **2** (a), (c)   **3** 1   **4** 90
5 -27 **6** 11   **7** 10   **8** (a) 1 (b) $\frac{1}{2}$ (c) $\frac{1}{2}$

Exercise 7a
1 0.67, 1.33 **2** 0.5, 2.5 **3** 0.75, 0.5 **4** 0.67, −0.67

Exercise 7b
1 (a) −2.4 or 3.4 (b) −2.55 or 3.55 **2** (a) $0.23 \leqslant x \leqslant 1.43$ (b) 0.25 or 1
3 (a) $x < -2.2$ or $-0.2 < x < 2.4$ (b) −2, −0.4 or 2.4

Exercise 8b
1 (a) $x + y \leqslant 20$ (b) $x + 3y \leqslant 32$ (c) $x \geqslant 10$
(d) $y \geqslant 4$ (e) $x \geqslant y + 2$ (f) $x \geqslant 2y$
(g) $4x + 5y \leqslant 75$
2 (a) $x \geqslant 50$ (b) $y \leqslant 20$ (c) $x + y \leqslant 40$
(d) $x + 2y \leqslant 200$ (e) $x \geqslant 3y$ (f) $x \geqslant y + 20$

Exercise 8c
1 8 of X and 10 of Y; 15 of X and none of Y
2 12 round, 15 square; 13 round, 14 square
3 $10x + 7y \leqslant 150$; $y > x$; $2y \leqslant 3x$; 8 dogs, 10 cats.

Exercise 9
1 (e) 5 (f) 0 **2** 45°, 45°, 90°

Exercise 10a
1 (a) closed; no identity element (b) commutative
(c) e.g. {1, 2}; e.g. {2, 4} (d) 3, 4
2 (a) Not associative (b) 0
3 (a) $D = \begin{pmatrix} -1 & -2 \\ 1 & 1 \end{pmatrix}$ (b) $\begin{pmatrix} 1 & 0 \\ 0 & 1 \end{pmatrix}$ (c) $\begin{pmatrix} -1 & 0 \\ 0 & -1 \end{pmatrix}$; $\begin{pmatrix} -1 & -2 \\ 1 & 1 \end{pmatrix}$

Exercise 10b
2 {1, 2, 3, 4}

Exercise 11
1 (a) 2 (b) 1 (c) $1\frac{1}{2}$ (d) 0 (e) 2 (f) 1
2 $f^{-1}: y \to y + 3$; $g^{-1}: y \to \dfrac{2}{y}$; $(fg)^{-1}: y \to \dfrac{2}{y + 3}$

Exercise 12a
1 (a) 3.4, 3, 2 (b) 3, $2\frac{1}{2}$, 1 (c) $1\frac{5}{6}$, $1\frac{1}{2}$, 1 (d) $2\frac{1}{2}$, $1\frac{1}{2}$, 0
2 (a) 3.4 (b) 0.34 (c) 23.4 (d) 983.4
3 3 **4** 1

Exercise 12b
1 (a) 59.14 (b) 62; 49; 390 **2** (a) 33.25 (b) 35; 14

Exercise 13a
1 (a) $\frac{4}{7}$ (b) $\frac{3}{7}$ **2** $\dfrac{x}{x + y}$ **3** (a) $\frac{1}{6}$ (b) $\frac{1}{3}$ **4** $\frac{1}{2}$
5 $\frac{1}{7}$

Exercise 13b
1 (a) $\frac{7}{15}$ (b) $\frac{1}{6}$ (c) $\frac{1}{3}$ (d) $\frac{7}{15}$ (e) $\frac{7}{15}$ (f) $\frac{7}{15}$; $\frac{7}{15}$
2 (a) $\frac{1}{75}$ (b) $\frac{8}{15}$ (c) $\frac{43}{75}$ (d) $\frac{32}{75}$ (e) $\frac{449}{1175}$ (f) $\frac{1}{675}$
3 (a) 0.49 (b) 0.09 (c) 0.42 (d) 0.1764 (e) 0.086

Exercise 14a
1 (a) Supplementary (b) Corresponding (c) Supplementary
(d) Alternate
3 36°, 72°, 72° or 45°, 45°, 90°   **3** 5.98 cm   **5** 75°

Exercise 14c
2 All are true

Exercise 15a
1 156°   **2** 20   **3** 16°

Exercise 15b
1 25 cm   **2** 17 cm, 12.7 cm   **3** Less than

Exercise 15c
1 76°, 52°, 38°   **2** 80°, 50°, 140°, 40°, 140°
3 92° and 80°, 50° and 44°   **4** 35°, 30°, 65°

Exercise 15d
1 (a) 3:4 (b) 3:7   **2** (a) 2:1 (b) 1:3 (c) 3:5 (d) 5:4
4 (a) 6080 km (b) 12160 km

Exercise 16
3 80°; 100°   **4** 34°

Exercise 17a
1 (a) 0.3649 (b) 0.8536 (c) 0.8816 (d) 0.7844 (e) 0.4746 (f) 3.0178
2 (a) 5.7° (b) 11.5° (c) 19.5° (d) 66.4° (e) 60° (f) 48.2°
(g) 35° (h) 38.7° (i) 53 1˄
3 (a) 6.04 cm, 5.25 cm   (b) 54.3°, 4.66 cm   (c) 33.6°, 6.63 cm
(d) 41.2°, 10.6 cm

Exercise 17b
1 (a) 4.7 cm (b) 7.31 cm (c) 8.14 cm (d) 13.7 cm   **2** (a) 16.9°
(b) 7.8°   **3** 7.82 km, 052°   **4** 12.9°   **5** 1.37 km, 2.92 km

Exercise 18a
1 8.89, 6.49   **2** 46.9° 93.1°, 11 5 cm; 6.9°, 1.4 cm   **3** 60°, 38°, 82°
4 10.4, 47°, 53°

Exercise 18b
1 3800 km   **2** 2910 km   **3** 15 640 km, 18 900 km

Exercise 18c

1 1.03 m   **2** 56°, 64°   **3** 14°

Exercise 19a

1 0.866, 0.5, −0.342, −0.866, −0.766
2 −0.5, −0.866, −0.940, −0.5, 0.643
3 −1.732, −0.577, 0.364, 1.732, −1.192
4 −0.5, 0.866, −0.577

Exercise 20a

1 (a) $\begin{pmatrix} 5 & -1 \\ 9 & 4 \end{pmatrix}$ (b) $\begin{pmatrix} -4 & -1 \\ -6 & 1 \end{pmatrix}$ (c) $\begin{pmatrix} 12 & -3 \\ 22 & 11 \end{pmatrix}$ (d) $\begin{pmatrix} 1 & -1 \\ 27 & 3 \end{pmatrix}$

    (e) $\begin{pmatrix} 6 & -3 \\ 14 & -2 \end{pmatrix}$ (f) $\begin{pmatrix} 1 \\ 17 \end{pmatrix}$ (g) $\begin{pmatrix} 6 \\ 13 \end{pmatrix}$ (h) $(0 \quad -5)$

    (i) $(1 \quad -1)$ (j) $\begin{pmatrix} 4 & -2 \\ 6 & -3 \end{pmatrix}$ (k) (1) (l) $\begin{pmatrix} 0 & -5 \\ 20 & 5 \end{pmatrix}$

2 −12, 16   **3** $-\frac{3}{2}$, −3   **4** 4, −8

6 $\begin{pmatrix} 283 \\ 461 \\ 532 \\ 354 \\ 604 \end{pmatrix}$ cost of postage each day; $(116 \quad 170)$, number of letters of each class posted that week; (2234), cost in pence of mail that week

7 $\begin{pmatrix} 1 & 1 & 0 & 0 \\ 1 & 0 & 1 & 0 \\ 0 & 1 & 1 & 1 \end{pmatrix}$; $\begin{pmatrix} 3 & 1 & 2 & 0 \\ 1 & 3 & 4 & 3 \end{pmatrix}$; there are two routes from A to Q

8 $\begin{pmatrix} 57 \\ 0 \end{pmatrix}$; $\begin{pmatrix} 69 \\ 0 \end{pmatrix}$

Exercise 20b

1 (a) 3   (b) 13   (c) 1   (d) −1   **2** (a) and (b)
3 (a) $\begin{pmatrix} \frac{3}{2} & -\frac{1}{2} \\ -2 & 1 \end{pmatrix}$ (b) $\begin{pmatrix} 2 & -1 \\ -5 & 3 \end{pmatrix}$ (c) $\begin{pmatrix} \frac{2}{11} & \frac{1}{11} \\ -\frac{5}{11} & \frac{3}{11} \end{pmatrix}$ (d) $\begin{pmatrix} \frac{1}{3} & -\frac{2}{3} \\ \frac{1}{12} & \frac{1}{3} \end{pmatrix}$

    (e) $\begin{pmatrix} \frac{1}{2} & 0 \\ 0 & \frac{1}{2} \end{pmatrix}$ (f) $\begin{pmatrix} 0 & -1 \\ -1 & 2 \end{pmatrix}$ **4** 3, 2   **5** $\frac{3}{5}$, $\frac{2}{5}$

6 (a) 3.2, −1.4   (b) −0.2, 1.4   (c) 0.3, −0.1
7 2, −1   **8** (a) 2, −1   (b) $-\frac{1}{7}$, $-\frac{4}{7}$ (c) $\frac{2}{7}$, $\frac{1}{7}$

Exercise 21

1 (a) (v)   (b) (ii)   **2** (ii)
3 Reflection of transformation made by **S** in $y = x$
4 Rotation about origin through $\tan^{-1}(\frac{4}{3})$, clockwise sense
5 Rotation about origin through 90°, clockwise sense. Shear parallel to x-axis.

Exercise 22a

1 (a) $\begin{pmatrix} 2 \\ 3 \end{pmatrix}$ (b) $\begin{pmatrix} 3 \\ 5 \end{pmatrix}$ (c) $\begin{pmatrix} -1 \\ -2 \end{pmatrix}$ (d) $\begin{pmatrix} 1 \\ 2 \end{pmatrix}$ (e) $\begin{pmatrix} 1 \\ -3 \end{pmatrix}$

2 (a) $2\sqrt{2}, 45°$ (b) $3\sqrt{2}, -45°$ (c) $\sqrt{2}, 135°$ (d) $2\sqrt{2}, -135°$
3 (a) $\sqrt{26}$ (b) $\sqrt{5}$ (c) $\sqrt{73}$ (d) 2 (e) $\sqrt{82}$
4 $\frac{1}{2}$ **5** $-\frac{1}{2}$ **6** 5, 7

Exercise 22b
1 (a) 1 (b) 1.73   **2** (a) 75° (b) 15°
3 1.81, 25°   **4** 106°   **5** (a) 2.65 (b) 41°

Exercise 22c
1 $\overrightarrow{BA} = \mathbf{a} - \mathbf{b}$ **2** 1:3   **4** $\binom{5}{7}$

Exercise 23a
1 (a) $12x^2$ (b) $20x^3 + 3$ (c) $20x^3$ (d) $6 - \dfrac{1}{x^2}$ (e) $\dfrac{6}{x^4}$
  (f) $4x + \dfrac{4}{x^5}$ **2** 2, (2, 4)

Exercise 23b
1 (a) $\frac{1}{3}x^3 + C$ (b) $x^4 + C$ (c) $x^7 + C$ (d) $\frac{6}{7}x^7 + C$
  (e) $x^4 + x^3 + C$ (f) $x^3 - \dfrac{1}{x} + C$ (g) $3x - \dfrac{1}{x} + C$
  (h) $x^2 + \dfrac{2}{x} + C$ (i) $\frac{3}{5}x^5 - \dfrac{1}{x^3} + C$ (j) $x^4 + \dfrac{2}{x^2} + C$

2 (a) $x^2 + 3x + C$ (b) $x^4 + x^3 + x^2 + C$ (c) $-\dfrac{1}{x} - \dfrac{1}{2x^2} + C$
3 $x^3 + x^2 + x - 1$ **4** 34   **5** $\frac{1}{2}$

Exercise 23c
1 (a) 511π (b) $\frac{1}{2}\pi$ (c) $\frac{28}{15}\pi$ **2** (a) $\frac{1}{2}\pi$ (b) $\frac{243}{5}\pi$ (c) $\frac{9}{2}\pi$

Exercise 23d
1 (a) min, -2 (b) max, 9 (c) max, 0; min, -4 (d) max, 1; min, $\frac{23}{27}$
2 (a) min, $(-1, -1)$ (b) max, $(-3, 12)$ (c) max $(4, 32)$;
     min $(0, 0)$ (d) max $(-1, 1)$; min $(1, -3)$

Exercise 23e
1 3 m s^{-1}; 6 m s^{-2} **2** 9 m s^{-1}: 2 m s^{-2}
3 8 m s^{-2}; 3 m; 17 m s^{-1}. 14 m   **4** 29 m s^{-1}, 10 m.

Index

Index

D. P. Baron and J. F. Connor
Economics £1.95

The contents of this Study Aid include: the economic problem and economic systems, organization of economic activity, population, location of industry, production. labour, unemployment, wages and trade unions, demand, supply a d price, money and banking, inflation, public finance, national income, international trade, the government and the economy.

A complete guide to preparing for O level, School Certificate and equivalent examinations in Economics.

L. E. W. Smith
English Language £1.75

The contents of this Study Aid include: composition, factual writing (including letter writing), summary, comprehension, grammar, direct and indirect speech, figures of speech and idiom, paraphrase, vocabulary, spelling and punctuation.

A complete guide to preparing for O level, School Certificate and equivalent examinations in English Language.

P. J. Hills and H. Barlow
Effective Study Skills £1.95

The contents of this Study Aid include: focusing attention and concentration, reading faster and more efficiently, finding information and using l braries, making notes, essay writing, punctuation and spelling, revision, taking an examination.

A complete guide to effective study, designed to help students eliminate indecision, anxiety and time-wasting and to introduce to them vital but often neglected techniques of study

Reference, language and information

☐	**Pan Dictionary of Synonyms and Antonyms**		£1.95p
☐	**Travellers' Multilingual Phrasebook**		£1.95p
☐	**Universal Encyclopaedia of Mathematics**		£2.95p

Literature guides

☐	**An Introduction to Shakespeare and his Contemporaries**	Marguerite Alexander	£2.95p
☐	**An Introduction to Fifty American Poets**	Peter Jones	£1.75p
☐	**An Introduction to Fifty Modern British Plays**	Benedict Nightingale	£2.95p
☐	**An Introduction to Fifty American Novels**	Ian Ousby	£1.95p
☐	**An Introduction to Fifty British Novels 1600–1900**	Gilbert Phelps	£2.50p
☐	**An Introduction to Fifty Modern European Poets**	John Pilling	£2.95p
☐	**An Introduction fo Fifty British Poets 1300–1900**	Michael Schmidt	£1.95p
☐	**An Introduction to Fifty Modern British Poets**		£2.95p
☐	**An Introduction to Fifty European Novels**	Martin Seymour-Smith	£1.95p
☐	**An Introduction to Fifty British Plays 1660–1900**	John Cargill Thompson	£1.95p

All these books are available at your local bookshop or newsagent, or can be ordered direct from the publisher. Indicate the number of copies required and fill in the form below   9

....

Name_____
(Block letters please)

Address_____

_____

Send to Pan Books (CS Department), Cavaye Place, London SW10 9PG
Please enclose remittance to the value of the cover price plus:
35p for the first book plus 15p per copy for each additional book ordered
to a maximum charge of £1.25 to cover postage and packing
Applicable only in the UK

While every effort is made to keep prices low, it is sometimes
necessary to increase prices at short notice. Pan Books reserve
the right to show on covers and charge new retail prices which
may differ from those advertised in the text or elsewhere